John Gould Fletcher
A Bibliography

John Gould Fletcher

A Bibliography

Bruce Morton

The Kent State University Press

The Serif Series: Number 37
Bibliographies and Checklists

Dean H. Keller, General Editor
Kent State University

Library of Congress Cataloging in Publication Data
Morton, Bruce,
      John Gould Fletcher, a bibliography.

      (The Serif series, bibliographies and
checklists; no. 37)
      Includes indexes.
      1.   Fletcher, John Gould, 1886–1950–Bibliography.
      I.   Title. II.   Series.
Z8304.13.M67   [PS3511.L457]   016.811'5'2
ISBN 0–87338–229–3   79–10897

Library of Congress Catalog Card Number 79–10897
ISBN 0–87338–229–3

Manufactured in the United States of America
at the press of the Oberlin Printing Company

I
dedicate
this
book
to
James Brunner
&
Harrison T. Meserole
each
a
teacher
and
friend
in
his
own
right.

Table of Contents

Acknowledgments

My thanks to the Inter-Library Loan departments of Dickinson College and Carleton College Libraries for their indefatigable and patient assistance. Special gratitude is due to Peter Dzwonkoski, Assistant Curator of the Collection of American Literature at the Beinecke Rare Book and Manuscript Library at Yale University, for assistance above and beyond the call. Also my thanks to Samuel A. Sizer, Curator of Special Collections, at the University of Arkansas for his helpful cooperation. To my wife, Barbara, for her patient support and in preparation of the indexing—thank you. In addition, my gratitude to Dickinson College and Carleton College for grants which made the preparation of manuscript possible.

I am particularly grateful to Mr. Booker T. Worthen and Mr. Ben D. Kimpel, Literary Executors of the Charlie May Fletcher Estate, for their permission to quote brief selections from Fletcher's work.

Finally, my thanks to the editors of the Serif Series, Kent State University Press, for their patient and helpful suggestions to me while preparing this bibliography.

Introduction

John Gould Fletcher occupies a unique place in our literature. No other writer is able to claim the distinction of having been involved in the Imagist movement of 1909–1925 and the Southern Agrarian movement of the 20s and 30s. Fletcher's participation in both of these literary movements is fascinatingly paradoxical; this alone whets the critical appetite. Both of these movements are important in the canon of twentieth-century American literature, therefore Fletcher's proximity and participation demand our attention. His reviews and essays provide us with an astute primary record of the literary and art worlds which swirled about him, and eventually passed him. So, too, does Fletcher's poetry reflect aspects of the literature which each of these movements or schools spawned.

Fletcher possessed an encyclopedic knowledge of the literature of Western Europe in addition to a wide knowledge of music and art. However, beyond recognition as a poet, he has received relatively little attention as a critic, or as an aesthetic and a social theoretician. These facets of the man and his work are worthy of attention in themselves, and ought not be overlooked, for they contribute to a truer understanding of his poetry.

John Gould Fletcher, above all else, was a poet. Artistically and emotionally, he was a poet. It was as a poet that he first made his mark on the literary scene,

when in May 1913 he concurrently published five books
of poetry with four different publishing houses. These
were followed by several more volumes between the
years 1915 and 1918 which were exemplary of the
experimentation taking place in the poetry "renaissance"
of the period. Fletcher's permutations of *vers libre* and use
of polyphonic prose received particular note from
contemporary critics. Although critical response was
mixed, as was to be the case throughout his career, he
was perceived as a poet of importance.

Throughout his thirty-seven year career Fletcher
would march to the beat of a different drum. Considered
by critics as avant-garde in his early work, especially
during the period of his association with the Imagists,
Fletcher was to find himself viewed during the later part
of his career as a saccharine proponent of Southern
regionalism. Whether or not this "standard" critical
perception which regards his career as one of unfulfilled
promise, as one of backsliding instead of evolution, is
correct remains to be authoritatively decided.

There is no doubt that the poet's return from Europe
to his native Arkansas during the early 30s had a
significance far beyond a mere change of domicile.
Philosophical precepts combined with artistic and
political chauvinism in motivating Fletcher's decision to
end his expatriation. For all the liberalism that the
Roosevelt administration's reaction to the economic crisis
of the 30s has had associated with it, officially in matters
of culture it propagated a conservative "return to roots"
policy. This attitude undoubtedly struck a sympathetic
chord in Fletcher, whose work, even during the later
Imagist period, evinced a tenor of "Americanism" and
regionalism. Such a total change in literary direction was
not at all peculiar just to him. Van Wyck Brooks, a

Fletcher correspondent, and preeminent literary critic for the previous two decades, underwent a similar evolution of literary focus at about this same time. I wish in no way to suggest that the parallel turns which Fletcher and Brooks made are in any manner directly related. They are not. They are, however, both representative of the tenor of the time. There was at this particular time need for introspection in America. A need to reaffirm what was *right* about the nation and the culture—a need to dispel doubt born by the Depression. Toward this end the WPA, through its artist's programs, officially encouraged the search for "a usable past." "The usable past" had for thirty years been a concept embraced by progressives. Van Wyck Brooks in particular had advocated such a search during his early career when he had castigated America as being, in a cultural sense, barren soil. And yet, in the 30s Brooks would be found winning a Pulitzer Prize for a literary history of New England which, in an impressionistic manner, praised the richness of our cultural heritage. And Fletcher who for a quarter of a century had willingly expatriated himself from his native land because he found it culturally bereft, now returned to sing its glories. Indeed, the restorative powers which a "sense of self" brings effect their results on both national and personal levels. In retrospect, it becomes apparent that Fletcher's transition from the Imagist innovator to regional poet is a manifestation of a shift in consciousness from an aesthetic frame of reference to one of cultural roots.

Heretofore, there has existed no adequate bibliographic resource which provides access to the wide range of verse and prose which Fletcher wrote, or to the biographical, critical, and scholarly secondary material which his work generated. It is my hope that this bibliography will help to alleviate this situation by offering itself as a guide to the collector, scholar, teacher, and student of John Gould Fletcher, the Imagist movement, and the Southern regionalist movement.

The user will note that the bibliography is organized into two main sections. The first section is devoted to works written by Fletcher, while the second section addresses itself to writings about Fletcher and his work. I have chosen not to include anthologies which contain Fletcher's poems. I have deviated from this decision only when the anthology is important in its own right, e.g., *The Imagist Anthology*, or *American Caravan*. It is my presumption that those wishing to survey Fletcher's anthologized work will be more than amply served by various editions of *Granger's Index to Poetry* and the *Chicorel Poetry Index*.

There are, no doubt, entries which I have failed to include because I remain unaware of them. There are others I have chosen not to include because they were of marginal relevance or lacked substance. Those who have indulged in bibliography well know that one uses the term "comprehensive" with qualification. However, I have made every effort to present a broadly "comprehensive" record of the career of John Gould Fletcher. My annotation is intended to provide the user with insight into the textual and contextual significance of each entry in an objective and noncritical manner. Therefore, individual poems have not been annotated because subjective interpretation is necessary. I am certain that there are instances of annotation where my objectivity has failed me, and that my own critical perception is reflected. I have tried to limit such occurrences.

It is my belief that bibliography should not be relegated to the status of merely being a "list" or "record." Certainly it is both of these things. Yet bibliography can appropriately serve a vital function in the study of a literary figure or literary movement. Not only does it offer a unique overview of the production of a writer's career, but it provides a graphic and substantive insight into trends of prolificacy, the stature of periodicals in which work was published, geographic trends in output and reception, trends in critical attention and critical reception. Toward this end, I have sustained, to the extent of utility, a chronological arrangement within each section of this book. Notable exceptions to chronological arrangement are sections II-A and II-B. Section II-A is arranged solely by alphabetization of author entry, whereas section II-B which contains reviews of Fletcher's books, retains chronological arrangement in regard to arrangement of books being reviewed, but within the context of the reviews for a particular book reverts to alphabetical author entry.

Above all else, it is my hope that bookmen, students, teachers, and scholars, each in their own way, will find this bibliographic offering accurate and useful to their particular endeavor.

Northfield, Minnesota
30 January 1978

I. Works By John Gould Fletcher

A. Monographs

1. *The Book of Nature*

> THE / BOOK OF NATURE / 1910-
> 1912 / BY / JOHN GOULD FLETCHER /
> LONDON / CONSTABLE AND COMPANY
> LTD / 1913

π^6 A-F^8 G^4 (G2^2 inserted) pp. [2] [i-vi] vii-x [1-3] 4-18 [19-21] 22-36 [37-39] 40-63 [64-67] 68-86 [87-89] 90-107 [108] [pp. *1-2*]: blank; [i]: half-title; [ii]: blank; [iii]: title; [iv]: blank; [v]: dedication; [vi]: blank; vii-x: contents list; [1]: Part I: The Months in Italy; [2]: blank; [3]: January: The Coming of the Snow; 4-5: February: The Winter Peace; 6: March: The Month of Storms; 7: April: The Blossoming; 8-9: May: The Coming of Summer; 10-11: June: Hymn to the Sun; 12: Interlude: The Storm; 13: July: The Month of the Sun; 14: August: The Month of the Moon; 15: September: The Harvest; 16: October: The North Wind's Gift; 17: November: The Burning of the Boughs; 18: December: The Hearth Festival; [19]: Part II: Sicilian Reeds: [20]: blank; [21]: Sea-Sounding Bells; 22: A Pantheist's Wish; 23-24: Lines Written at Taormina, Sicily; 25: Song of the Summer Breezes; 26: The Secret of the Hills; 27: Summer Silence; 28-29: The Bacchanal; 30-32: The Dead City (Messina, 1908-1911); 33-34: Girgenti; 35-36: The Flocks of Pan; [37]: Part III: England; [38]: blank; [39]-40: The Cry of Nature; 41: Lines Written at Stonehenge; 42: Midsummer Dawn at Sea; 43: To a Skylark; 44: On a Hillside; 45-46: In the Wood; 47: Full Moon; 48: Sun After Rain; 49: Haze on the Hills; 50: Death of the Summer, 1912; 51: Epitaph on the Summer of 1912; 52: The Summons of Autumn; 53-54: A Song of Autumn; 55-56: The Wind's Booty; 57: Summer's Souvenir; 58-59: A Ballad of Dead Autumns; 60: Voices of the Wind; 61: Midwinter Sunset; 62-63: Nature's Death; [64]: blank; [65]: Part IV: Italy—Bavaria—Switzerland—Provence—America; [66]: blank; [67]: Venice; 68: The Voice in the Pines; 69: The Lure of Evening; 70-71: Rome; 72-73: Cypresses; 75: Valley and Park; 75: Golden Leaves; 76: The Voice of the Torrent; 77: Alpine Violets;

78: Voices; 79-80: The Home of Memory; 81-82: The Woman of the Mountains; 83: Provence; 84: Song of the Sun-Intoxicated; 85: Midsummer; 86: Night in the Wilderness; [87]: Part V: Two Days at Versailles; [88]: blank; [89]-96: 19th May 1912; [89]-90: I. The Poppy Song; 91: II. The Sadness of Summer; 92: III. To a Rose of the Trianon; 93: IV. By the Fountain; 94: V. Voices in the Wood; 95: VI. The Fountains of Sunset; 96: VII. Midsummer Twilight; 97-104: 21st October 1912; 97-98: I. Epilogue to the Poppy Song; 99: II. Autumn Elegy; 100: III. To a Rose of the Autumn; 101: IV. By the Fountain; 102: V. Voices of Autumn; 103: VI. Autumn Evening; 104: VII. Farewell to Versailles; 105: Epilogue to "Two Days at Versailles"; 106-107: Epilogue to "The Book of Nature"; [108]: colophon

Bound in blue cloth; spine stamped in gold; front has a frame of double rules stamped on it. Endpapers white. Top edges trimmed and gilt; fore and bottom edges untrimmed.

Note: Poems. This is one of five volumes which Fletcher published in May 1913, at his own expense. The poet attempts to imitate the style of the Georgians.

2. *The Dominant City (1911-1912)*

THE DOMINANT / CITY (1911-1912) / BY JOHN GOULD FLETCHER / LONDON: MAX GOSCHEN LTD. / 20, GREAT RUSSELL STREET, W.C. / MCMXIII

[A]⁸ B-E⁸[i-ii] [1-6] 7-75 [76-78]

[i]: half-title; [ii]: blank; [1]: title; [2]: [blank; [3]: dedication; [4]: blank; [5-6]: contents list; 7: The Dominant City; 8: The Hoardings; 9-10: The Deserted Factory; 11: The Evening Clouds; 12: London Evening; 13: Pleasure's Awakening; 14-16: The Night of Pleasure; 17-18: Eros; 19: Song of Night; 20-22: London at Night; 23-25: In the City of Night; 26: Tragic Night; 27: Triumphant Night; 28: The Hour of Peace; 29: Saturday Night: Horses Going to Pasture; 30: The Great Moon; 31: In the Night; 32: From the Night to the Dawn; 33: Dawn; 34: The Clouds; 35: Factory Chimneys; 36: Back Streets; 37: Joy; 38: The Age of Steel; 39: Twilight; 40-43: Chorus for the Tragedy of Man; 44: Midwinter Moon Over the City; 45: Dawn In Italy and In London; 46: Saturday Night in Fleet Street; 47: At the Meeting of the Days; 48: Banners; 49: The Magicians; 50: The Forces at Work In

the City; 51: The Forging of the Sun; 52: Autumn Sunset; 53-54: Two Autumn Dawns; 55: An Autumn Picture; 56: The City Lies at Ease Upon the Night; 57-59: The Litanies of the City; 60-63: The Death of the City; 64-66: The Anarchist's Dream; 67-69: Coal; 70-73: The Sower; 74-75: Epilogue: The Prayer; [76]: colophon; [77-78]: blank

Bound in brown paper covered boards; spine and front stamped in gold. Endpaper white. All edges trimmed; variant copies have top edge untrimmed.

Note: Poems. This is one of the five volumes which Fletcher published in May 1913, at his own expense. Of these five volumes this is the most original and ambitious, an attempt to capture the essence of the modern city. The poet's form is dictated largely by the influence of Baudelaire and Verhaeren.

3. *Fire and Wine*

FIRE AND WINE / BY / JOHN GOULD FLETCHER / [ornament] / LONDON / GRANT RICHARDS LTD. / PUBLISHERS [Copyright page:] THE RIVERSIDE PRESS LIMITED, / EDIN-BURGH /1913

[A]⁸ B-E⁸ [1-6] 7-9 [10-12] 13-37 [38-40] 41-75 [76-80]

[i]: half-title; [2]: blank; [3]: title; [4]: The Riverside Press Limited, Edinburgh 1913; [5]: dedication; [6]: blank; 7-9: contents list; [10]: blank; [11]: Book I. Fire: [12]: blank; 13: Spring Love; 14: Midsummer Love; 15: Autumnal Love; 16-17: Midwinter Love; 18: I Cannot Love You; 19: Lacking Your Love; 20: In the Year That is Past; 21: Could My Soul Dream; 22: Eyes; 23: Hands; 24: Mystic Union; 25: Song In the Desert; 26: Love and Suspicion; 27: The End of Love; 28: The Icy Waters; 29: In the Shadow of a Pine; 30-31: A Prayer Answered; 32: At Parting; 33: The Mating; 34: Love's Memory Fading; 35: Love's Memory Forgotten; 36: The End of Desire; 37: The Final Futility; [38]: blank; [39]: Book II. Wine; [40]: blank; 41: To My Mother; 42-43: The Vowels (To Leon Bakst); 44: The Three Transformations of Poetry; 45: The Hosts of Song; 46: Dionysus and Apollo; 47: The Poet's Character; 48: The Poet's Desire; 49: Poetic Art; 50: On an Editor's Refusal of My Poems; 51: To the Publisher Who Refused to Publish My Poems; 52: The Poet's Autumn; 53: The Poet's Immortality; 54-55: Lines to the Admirers of Alfred Stevens (On

the Occasion of the Memorial Exhibition of His Works); 56: To
the Public; 57: Present-Day Poetry; 58-59: Clown's Song; 60: The
Price of Poetry; 61: Art's Sacrifices; 62: Fatigue; 63-64; The
Dream of Art; 65-66: A Distant Song; 67: Dream-Poetry; 68-69:
Art; 70: To the Muse; 71: The Poet I; 72: Time and Poet; 73-74:
The Poet II; 75: The Triumph of Song; [76-80]: blank

    Bound in green cloth; spine and front stamped in gold.
Endpapers white. Top edges trimmed and gilt; fore and bottom
edges untrimmed.

Note: Poems. This is one of five volumes which Fletcher published
in May 1913, at his own expense. These poems are primarily
about imaginary loves and poetry in general.

4. *Fool's Gold*

FOOL'S GOLD / BY JOHN GOULD FLETCHER / LONDON: MAX GOSCHEN LTD. / 20, GREAT RUSSELL STREET, W.C. / MCMIII

    [A]⁸ B-F̄⁸ [i-ii] [1-8] 9-41 [42-44] 45-91 [92]

    [i]: half-title; [ii]: blank; [1]: title; [2]: Rejoice in misery, solitude,
and misfortune, for out of these comes strength, courage and
deliverance; [3]: In Memoriam; [4]: blank; [5-6]: contents list; [7]:
Part I: The Search; [8]: blank; 9: Prelude; 10: Contradiction; 11:
Hope; 12: Ambition; 13: Drunkeness; 14: Discontent; 15-16:
Failure; 17: Life; 18: Freedom; 19: Knowledge; 20-21: Sorrow; 22-
23: Loneliness; 24: Attainment; 25: Faith; 26-27: Blasphemy; 28-
29: Indifference; 30: Sin; 31-32: Resignation; 33: Despair; 34:
Ennui; 35: To Death; 36: In Sickness; 37: Aspiration; 38: At the
Gate of Death; 39: In the Hour of Death; 40: Death; 41:
Greatness; [42]: blank; [43]: Part II: The Discovery; [44]: blank;
45: Recovery; 46: Achievement and Failure; 47: Impossible
Silence; 48: The Weary Hours; 49: Resolution; 50: Perhaps; 51:
Revolt; 52: What Matters?; 53-54: England; 55-58: Vanity of
Vanities; 59: "Truth Dies—"; 60: Why I Laugh; 61: Fear; 62: The
Truth of the Matter; 63: The Golden Demon; 64: Reconciliation;
65: What the Wind Sang; 66: The Wisdom of a Fool; 67-68: Evil
and Good; 69-70: The Mother's Thought of Her Son; 71: The
Father's Thought of His Daughter; 72: The Idiot; 73: Failure; 74:
To Those Who Fail; 75: Rocket Ascending; 76: The Rocket Falling
77: My Confession; 78: Recrudescence; 79: Satiety; 80-81: The

Two Leaves; 82: Written on the Top of the Great St. Bernard
Pass; 83: Written at the Grand Chartreuse; 84: England Again;
85: The Lamp of Parliament; 86: An English Newspaper; 87: After
Breakfasting; 88: Marriage; 89: From the Depths; 90: The Last
Judgment; 91: Conclusion; [92]: colophon
   Bound in brown paper covered boards; spine and front stamped
in gold. Endpapers white. All edges trimmed.
Note: Poems. This is one of five volumes which Fletcher published
in May 1913, at his own expense. The theme throughout is
personal experience and one begins to detect the author's
increasingly pessimistic attitude and disillusionment with life.

5. *Visions of the Evening*

VISIONS OF / THE EVENING / BY / JOHN G.
FLETCHER / LONDON / ERSKINE MAC-
DONALD / 17 Surrey Street, W.C. / 1913

[A-F]⁴ [i-iv] 1-43 [44]

   [i]: title; [ii]: blank; [iii-iv]: contents list; 1-2: To the Immortal
Memory of Charles Baudelaire; 3-4: Invocation to Evening; 5:
Invocation to Solitude; 6: Invocation to Night; 7: The Lover of
Solitude; 8: The Valley of Kashmir; 9: The Irony of Night; 10:
Towards the Impossible; 11: I Contemplate My Toil; 12: Vision
After Midnight; 13: Futility; 14: My Hours; 15: Anatomy of
Myself; 16: The Albatross; 17: The Caged Eagle; 18: Misfortune;
19: Golgotha; 20: The Descent Into Hell; 21: Midnight Prayer; 22:
Remembrances (To Maurice Ravel); 23: The Lid; 24: On a Windy
Day; 25: Woman (To J. D. Fergusson); 26: From the Japanese; 27:
From the Chinese; 28: The Mystic Vision; 29: Adrift; 30-31:
Clouds; 32: The Body to the Soul; 33: Dead Thoughts; 34: Day
and Night; 35: Greatness and Littleness; 36: The Everlasting
Paradox; 37: Dreams; 38: The Songs of Silence; 39: Summer
Sleep; 40: End of the Revel; 41: The Smoke of Dreams; 42: My
Grave (June 17, 1910); 43: My Monument (December 25, 1912);
[44]: colophon
   Bound in blue cloth; spine and front stamped in gold.
Endpapers white. All edges trimmed.
Note: Poems. This is one of five volumes which Fletcher published
in May 1913, at his own expense. Technically this volume
represents an approach to poetry closer to that of the French
symbolists than anything Fletcher had heretofore attempted.

6. *Irradiations Sand and Spray*

IRRADIATIONS / SAND AND SPRAY / BY /
JOHN GOULD FLETCHER / [ornament] /
BOSTON AND NEW YORK / HOUGHTON
MIFFLIN COMPANY / The Riverside Press
Cambridge / 1915

[A-K]⁴ [i-viii] ix-xiv [xv-xviii] [1-2] 3-39 [40-42] 43-59 [60-62]

[i]: half-title; [ii]: blank; [iii]: title; [iv]: copyright page; [v]: dedication; [vi]: blank; [vii]: acknowledgment; [viii]: blank; ix-[xv]: preface; [xvi]: blank; [xvii]: contents list; [xviii]: blank; [1]: Irradiations; [2]: blank; 3: I; 4: II; 5: III; 6: IV; 7: V; 8: VI; 9: VII; 10: VIII; 11: IX; 12: X; 13: XI; 14: XII; 15: XIII; 16: XIV; 17: XV; 18: XVI; 19: XVII; 20: XVIII; 21: XIX; 22: XX; 23: XXI; 24: XXII; 25: XXIII; 26: XXIV; 27: XXV; 28: XXVI; 29: XXVII; 30: XXXIII; 31: XXIX; 32: XXX; 33: XXXI; 34: XXXII; 35: XXXIII; 36: XXXIV; 37: XXXV; 38-39: XXXVI; [40]: Epilogue; [41]: Sand and Spray. A Sea Symphony; [42]: blank; 43-44: Part I. The Gale; 45: Part II. Variations (1) Sailboats; 46-47: (2) The Tide; 48: (3) The Sands; 49: (4) The Gulls; 50-51: (5) Steamers; 52: (6) Night of Stars; 53-54: Part III. Variations (1) The Groundswell; 55: (2) Snow at Sea; 56: (3) The Night Wind; 57: (4): The Wreck; 58: (5) Tide of Storms; 59-[60]: Part IV. The Calm; [61-62]: blank

Bound in green paper wrappers folded over and attached at spine to boards; spine has black lettering and front black lettering and publishers ornament. Endpapers white. All edges trimmed. *Note*: Poems. Many of these poems first appeared in *Poetry* and *Egoist*. The influence of Mallarmé, Gauguin, and Debussy is detectable. The preface to this volume attempts to explain the methodology and theory of the poems contained therein. "The New Poetry Series" on front cover. (See I-A-6-a.)

6.a. *Irradiations and Spray.*

IRRADIATIONS / SAND AND SPRAY / BY /
JOHN GOULD FLETCHER / London /
CONSTABLE & CO. LIMITED / BOSTON AND NEW
YORK / HOUGHTON MIFFLIN COMPANY / 1915

[A-K]⁴ [i-viii] ix-xiv [1-2] 3-39 [40-42] 43-59 [60-62]

[i]; half-title; [ii]: blank; [iii]: title; [iv]: blank; [v]: dedication; [vi]:

blank; [vii]: acknowledgment; [viii]: blank; iv-[xv]: preface; [xvi]:
blank; [xvii]: contents list; [xviii]: blank; [1]-[62]: same as
American edition (See I-A-6).

Bound in rose paper wrappers folded over and attached at spine
to boards; spine has black lettering and front black lettering with
publishers ornament. Endpapers white. All edges trimmed.
Note: Poems. This is the British issue of I-A-6 with new title page.

7. *Goblins and Pagodas*

GOBLINS AND PAGODAS / BY / JOHN GOULD
FLETCHER / [ornament] / BOSTON AND NEW
YORK / HOUGHTON MIFFLIN COMPANY / The
Riverside Press Cambridge / 1916

[A-H]⁸ [i-viii] ix-xxi [xxii] xxiii-xxiv [xxv-xxvi] [1-2] 3 [4] 5-9
[10] 11-15 [16] 17-20 [21-24] 25-29 [30] 31-37 [38] 39-44 [45] 46-
51 [52] 53-60 [61] 62-65 [66] 67-73[74] 75-80 [81] 82-85 [86] 87-
91 [92] 93-98 [99-100]

[i]: half-title; [ii]: blank; [iii]: title; [iv]: copyright page; [v]:
dedication; [vi]: blank; [vii]: acknowledgment; [viii]: blank; ix-
[xxii]: preface; xxiii-[xxv]: contents list; [xxvi]: blank; [1]: Section
I: The Ghosts of an Old House; [2]: blank; 3-[4]: Prologue; 5-[10]:
Part I. The House; 5: Bedroom; 6: Library; 6-7: Indian Skull; 7:
Old Nursery; 8: The Back Stairs; 9: The Wall Cabinet; 9-[10]: The
Cellar; [10]: The Front Door; 11-[16]: Part II. The Attic; 11-12: In
the Attic; 12: The Calendar in the Attic; 13: The Hoopskirt; 14:
The Little Chair; 14-15: In the Dark Corner; 15-[16]: The Toy
Cabinet; [16]: The Yardstick; 17-[21]: Part III. The Lawn; 17: The
Three Oaks; 18: An Oak; 18-19: Another Oak; 19-20: The Old
Barn; 20: The Well; 20-[21]: The Trees; [21]: Vision; [22]:
Epilogue; [23]: Section II: Symphonies; [24]: blank; 25-[30]: Blue
Symphony; 31-[38]: Solitude in the City (Symphony in Black and
Gold); 31-32: Words At Midnight; 32-34: the Evening Rain; 34-
35: Street of Sorrows; 35-[38]: Song in the Darkness; 39-[45]:
Green Symphony; 46-[52]: Golden Symphony; 53-[61]: White
Symphony; 62-[66]: Midsummer Dreams (Symphony in White
and Blue); 67-[74]: Orange Symphony; 75-[81]: Red Symphony;
82-[86]: Violet Symphony; 87-[92]: Grey Symphony; 93-[99]:
Poppies of the Red Year (A Symphony in Scarlet); [100]: colophon

Bound in printed green wrappers folded over and attached at

spine to boards; black lettering on front. Endpapers white. All
edges trimmed; variant copies—edges untrimmed.
Note: Poems. "Ghosts of an Old House" and the color
symphonies brought together in one volume. In his preface the
author makes an elaborate effort to explain his theory and
method through the use of concepts usually associated with music
and the visual arts.

8. *Japanese Prints*

[all within double rules] *Japanese Prints / By / John
Gould Fletcher / With Illustrations By / Dorothy Pulis
Lathrop /* [printer's device] */ Boston / The Four Seas
Company / 1918*

[A-F] 8 [1-10] 11-17 [18-20] 21-37 [38-40] 41-60 [61-62] 63-75
[76-78] 79-94 [95-96]

[1]: half-title; [2]: [other works] by John Gould Fletcher;
[plate and opaque overlay tipped in]; [3]: title; [4]: copyright
page; [4]: dedication; [5]: blank; [6-9]: contents list; [10]: blank;
11-17:preface; [18]: blank; [19]: [illustration] Part I; [20]: blank;
21: Lovers Embracing; 22: A Picnic Under the Cherry Trees;
23: Court Lady Standing Under Cherry Tree; 24: Court Lady
Standing Under a Plum Tree; 25: A Beautiful Woman; 26: A
Reading; 27: An Actor as a Dancing Girl; 28: Josan No Miya;
29: An Oiran and her [*sic*] Kamuso; 30: Two Ways of Love; 31:
Kurenai-ye or "Red Picture"; 32: A Woman Standing by a Gate
with an Umbrella; 33: Scene from a Drama; 34: A Woman in
Winter Costume; 35: A Pedlar; 36: Kiyonobu and Kiyomasu
Contrasted; 37: An Actor [illustration]; [38]: blank; [39]:
[illustration] Part II; [40]: blank; 41: Memory and Forgetting;
42: Pillar-Print, Masonobu; 43: The Young Daimyo; 44:
Masonobu-Early; 45: The Beautiful Geisha; 46: A Young Girl
[plate and opaque overlay tipped in]; 47: The Heavenly Poetess;
48: The Old Love and the New; 49: Fugitive Thoughts; 50:
Disappointment; 51: The Traitor; 52: The Fop; 53: Changing
Love; 54: In Exile; 55: The True Conquerer; 56: Spring Love;
57: The Endless Lament; 58: Toyonobu. Exile's Return [plate
and opaque overlay tipped in]; 59: Wind and Chrysanthemum;
60: The Endless Pilgrimage; [61]: [illustration] Part III; [62]:
blank; 63: The Clouds; 64: Two Ladies Contrasted; 65: A Night
Festival; 66: Distant Coasts; 67: On the Banks of the Sumida;
68: Yoshiwara Festival; 69: Sharaku Dreams; 70: A Life [plate

and opaque overlay tipped in]; 71: Dead Thoughts; 72: A
Comparison; 73: Mutability; 74: Despair; 75: The Lonely Grave
[illustration]; [76]: blank; [77]: [illustration] Part IV; [78]: blank;
79: Evening Sky; 80: City Lights; 81: Fugitive Beauty; 82: Silver
Jars; 83: Evening Rain; 84: Toy-Boxes; 85: Moods; 86: Grass;
87: A Landscape; 88: Terror; 89: Mid-Summer Dusk; 90:
Evening Bell from a Distant Temple; 91: A Thought; 92: The
Stars; 93: Japan; 94: Leaves [illustration]; [95]: blank; [96]: An
edition of 1000 copies only, of which 975 copies have been
printed on Olde Style paper, and 25 copies on Japanese Vellum.

Bound in green cloth; stamped in gold on spine and front.
Endpapers beige with brown drawings. Top edges, trimmed and
gilt; fore bottom edges untrimmed.
Note: Poems. Intended by the author to be verse commentary on
life and manners with an underlying philosophy of Zen
Buddhism. Fletcher "defines" his "doctrine" in the preface.
Norman Holmes Pearson, a personal friend of Fletcher, stated
that Fletcher had never seen a copy of this book on Japanese
vellum. There are no known copies of the book on Japanese
vellum.

9. *The Tree of Life*

THE TREE OF LIFE / BY / JOHN GOULD
FLETCHER / "And the tree of life was in the midst of
the garden" / LONDON / CHATTO & WINDUS /
1918

[A]⁸B-H⁸ [i-vi] vii-viii [ix] 10-12 [13] 14-34 [35] 36-58 [59] 60-
81 [82-83] 84-127 [128]

[i]: half-title; [ii]: blank; [iii]: title; [iv]: blank; [v]: dedication;
[vi]: blank; vii-viii: contents list; [ix-12]: Preludes; 10: Strophe;
10-11: Antistrophe; 11-12: Epode; [13]: Book I: The Aster
Flower; 14-15: Memory: The Walk on the Beach; 16-17: The
Walk in the Garden; 18: The Aster Flower; 19-20: Autumnal
Clouds; 21: Night Song; 22: Night Song; 23-24: Three Nights;
25: The Dahlias; 26: The Conflict; 27: The Ordeal; 28: The
Vision; 29: The Conquest; 30: Faith; 31: The Silence; 32: After
Parting; 33-34: Reunion; [35]: Book II: Fruit of Flame; 36-37:
The Voyage; 38-39: On the Beach; 40-43: The Second Walk in
the Garden; 44-45: In the Open Air; 46: In the House; 47-48:
On the Verandah; 49-51: The Parting; 52: After; 53-54: In the

Garden of Dreams; 55: The Empty House; 56-57: The Offering;
58: The Return to Life; [59]: Book III: From Empty Days; 60-63:
Part I. The Tree of Life; 64-67: Part II. Alone in the Garden;
68-71: Part III. Love and Death; 72-76: Part IV. The Empty
Days; 77-81: Part V. The Last Battle; [82]: blank; [83]: Book IV:
Dreams in the Night; 84-85: The Coming of Night; 87: The
New Life; 88: The Sky-Garden; 89-90: The Onset; 91: The
Crisis; 92: Failure; 93-94: Disunion; 95-97: The Night of
Renunciation; 98-100: In Memory of a Night; 101-102:
Epilogue; [103]: Book V: Towards the Darkness; 104: Falling
Leaves; 105: Autumn Sunset; 106-107: Ebb-tide; 108-109: The
Walk in the City; 110: The Everlasting Flower; 111: Song of
Parting; 112: Second Song of Parting; 113-14: November
Days; 115-117: Three Nights; 118: The Last Coals; 119: The
Harvest; 120: The Final Doubt; 121-122: Reunion; 123-124:
Postludes; 123: Strophe; 123-124: Antistrophe; 124: Epode;
125-127: Epilogue: Midwinter Love; [128]: colophon
   Bound in blue cloth; spine and front stamped in gold.
Endpapers gray. Edges trimmed; top edges gilt. Variant copies
with fore and bottom edges untrimmed.
Note: Poems. Originally titled "Love's Tragedy" in manuscript
form. The author belived that this book would serve as an
excellent introduction to the kind of poetry which he was trying
to produce.

10. *La Poésie d' André Fontainas*
   [cover] John Gould FLETCHER / [horizontal
   rule] / La Poésie d' André Fontainas / [horizontal
   rule] / LE MONDE NOUVEAU / 25, Rue Boisie-
   vent, 25 / PARIS (X V I 8) / [ornament] / 1919 / [orna-
   ment]
      [A]6 [i-ii] [1] 2-10
      [i]: half-title; [ii]: blank; [1]-10: La Poésie d'André Fontainas
      Bound pamphlet style in buff colored paper with brown
   lettering.
   Note: Critical essay. Text in French. See "The Poetry of André
   Fontainas" *New World*, 1 (June-July 1919), 258-69, (I-B-91).

11. *Breakers and Granite*

Breakers and Granite / BY / JOHN GOULD
FLETCHER / Author of "The Tree of Life" / NEW
YORK / THE MACMILLAN COM-
PANY / 1921 / All rights reserved.

[A-L]⁸ [i-xii] 1-163 [164]

[i]: blank; [ii]: blank; [iii]: half-title; [iv]: printer's device; [v]:
title; [vi]: copyright page; [vii]: dedication; [viii]: blank; [ix]:
acknowledgment; [x]: blank; [xi-xii]: contents lists; 1-4: The
Arrival; 5-7: New York; 8-14: Manhattan; 15-16: Skyscrapers;
17-25: New York Sketches; 17-18: Overlooking the Hudson,
Autumn; 19: Central Park; 20-21: Broadway's Canyon; 22-23:
The Alleyways; 24: Old Jewish Cemetery; 25: Longue Vue; 26-
29: New England Sunset; 30-31: New England Winter; 32-34:
The Empty House; 35-41: Clipper-Ships; 42-43: Lake Shore at
Night; 44-48: The Building of Chicago; 49-57: Down the
Mississippi; 49-50: Embarkation; 51: Heat; 52: Full Moon; 53-
54: The Moon's Orchestra; 55: The Stevedores; 56: Night
Landing; 57: The Silence; 58-63: The Old South; 64-78: The
Great River; 79-89: Gettysburg; 90-94: The Passing of the
South; 95-99: The Grand Canyon of the Colorado; 100-113:
Arizona Poems; 100-101: The Well in the Desert; 102-104:
Mexican Quarter; 105-106: Cliff Dwelling; 107-108: The
Windmills; 109-111: The Fuel Vendor; 112-113: Rain in the
Desert; 114-116: The Song of the Wind; 117-126: The Passing
of the West; 127-139: Songs of Arkansas; 127-130: Invocation;
131-132: Women's Song; 133-137: War-Song; 138-139: Death-
Song; 140-143: In the City of Night (To the Memory of Edgar
Allan Poe); 144-149: America 1916; 150-157: The Poem of
Mist; 159-163: Lincoln; [164]: blank

January 1921 issue bound in blue paper covered board; gold
lettering. March 1921 issue bound in olive green cloth; spine
lettered in black. Remainder binding of March 1921 issue is
pea-green cloth with spine lettered in black. Endpapers white.
All edges trimmed.

Note: Poems and prose poems. Many of these poems had been
previously published in various periodicals. Much of the material
contained herein deals with the poet's impressions of his native
America.

12. *Paul Gauguin: His Life and Art*

PAUL GAUGUIN / His Life and Art / BY / JOHN GOULD FLETCHER / *WITH TEN IL-LUSTRATIONS* / [ornament] / NICHOLAS L. BROWN / NEW YORK MCMXXI

[A-M]8 [i-ii] [plate] [1-10] 11-14 [plate] 15-30 [plate] 31-47 [48] 49-54 [plate] 55-62 [plate] 63-94 [plate] 95-110 [plate] 111-115 [116] 117-126 [plate] 127-142 [plate] 143-158 [plate] 159-193 [194]

[i]: half-title; [ii]: Uniform with this volume: NOA NOA. By Paul Gauguin Translated from the French by O. F. Theis. With ten illustrations in half tone. $2.00; [plate]: Self-portrait of Gauguin; [1]: title; [2]: copyright page; [3]: dedication; [4]: quote; [5]: contents list; [6]: blank; [7]: list of illustrations; [8]: blank; [9]: PAUL GAUGUIN; [10]: blank; 11-14 [plate: Portrait of Gauguin's Mother] 15-30 [plate: The Painter Schuffenecker and His Family] 31-47: Part I: The Formation 1849-1885; [48]: blank; 49-54 [plate: Struggle of Jacob with the Angel] 55-62 [plate: The Idol] 63-74: Part II: The Struggle with Impressionism 1885-1889; 75-94 [plate: Tahitian Women] 95-110 [plate: Hina Maruru (Feast to Hina) 111-115: Part III: The School of Pont-Aven 1889-1891; [116]: blank; 117-126 [plate: The Old Spirit] 127-142 [plate: Calvary] 143-152: Part IV: The Return to Savagery 1891-1895; 153-158 [plate: Matamua (Olden Days)] 159-191: Part V: The Fight Against Civilization 1895-1903; 192-193: Bibliography of Works Consulted; [194]: blank

Bound in brown paper covered boards with linen backing; brown label on spine with black lettering. Endpapers gray. All edges trimmed.

Note: Biography. Fletcher sensed in Gauguin something akin to his own feeling of exile, as well as a spirit compatible with his own revolt and disgust with nineteenth-century progressive civilization.

13. *Preludes and Symphonies*

PRELUDES AND / SYMPHONIES / BY / JOHN
GOULD FLETCHER / [ornament] / BOSTON
AND NEW YORK / HOUGHTON MIFFLIN
COMPANY / THE RIVERSIDE PRESS CAMBRIDGE / 1922

[A-K]⁸ [L]⁶ [i-ix] x-xi [xii] [1-2] 3-39 [40-42] 43-59 [60] [1-2] 3
[4] 5-9 [10] 11-15 [16] 17-20 [21-24] 25-29 [30] 31-37 [38] 39-
44 [45] 46-51 [52] 53-60 [61] 62-65 [66] 67-73 [74] 75-80 [81]
82-85 [86] 87-91 [92] 93-98 [99-100]

[i]: half-title; [ii]: blank; [iii]: title; [iv]: copyright page; [v]:
dedication; [vi]: blank; [vii]: note; [viii]: blank; [ix]-[xii]:
contents list; [1]: Irradiations; [2]: blank; 3: I; 4: II; 5: III; 6: IV;
7: V; 8: VI; 9: VII; 10: VIII; 10: VIII; 11: IX; 12: X; 13: XI; 14: XII;
15: XIII; 16: XIV; 17: XV; 18: XVI; 19: XVII; 20: XVIII; 21: XIX;
22: XX; 23: XXI; 24: XXII; 25: XXIII; 26: XXIV; 27: XXV; 28:
XXVI; 29: XXVII; 30: XXVIII; 31: XXIX; 32: XXX; 33: XXXI; 34:
XXXII; 35: XXXIII; 36: XXXIV; 37: XXXV; 38-39: XXXVI; [40]:
Epilogue; [41]: Sand and Spray: A Sea-Symphony; [42]: blank; 43-
44: Part I. The Gale; 45-52: Part II. Variations; 45: Sailboats; 46-
47: The Tide; 48: The Sands; 49: The Gulls; 50-51: Steamers; 52:
Night of Stars; 53-58: Part III. Variations; 53-54: The
Groundswell; 55: Snow at Sea; 56: The Night Wind; 57: The
Wreck; 58: Tide of Storms; 59-[60]: Part IV. The Calm; [1]:
Section I: The Ghosts of an Old House; [2]: blank; 3-[4]: Prologue;
5-[10]: Part I. The House; 5: Bedroom; 6: Library; 6-7: Indian
Skull; 7: Old Nursery; 8: The Backstairs; 9: The Wall Cabinet; 9-
[10]: The Cellar; [10]: The Front Door; 11-[16]: Part II. The Attic;
11-12: In the Attic; 12: The Calendar in the Attic; 13: The
Hoopskirt; 14: The Little Chair; 14-15: In the Dark Corner; 15-
[16]: The Toy Cabinet; [16]: The Yardstick; 17-[21]: Part III. The
Lawn; 17: The Three Oaks; 18: An Oak; 18-19: Another Oak; 19-
20: The Old Barn; 20: The Well; 20-[21]: The Trees; [22]:
Epilogue; [23]: Section II: Symphonies; [24]: blank; 25-[30]: Blue
Symphony; 31-[38]: Solitude in the City (Symphony in Black and
Gold); 31-32: Words at Midnight; 32-34: The Evening Rain; 34-
35: Street of Sorrows; 36-[38]: Song in the Darkness; 39-[45]:
Green Symphony; 46-[52]: Golden Symphony; 53-[61]: White
Symphony; 62-[66]: Midsummer Dreams (Symphony in White
and Blue); 67-[74]: Orange Symphony; 75-[81]: Red Symphony;
82-[86]: Violet Symphony; 87-[92]: Grey Symphony; 93-[99]:

Poppies of the Red Year (A Symphony in Scarlet); [100]: blank
   Bound in green paper boards; spine has black lettering and
front has black lettering and bears publishers ornament in
black. Endpapers white. Top edges trimmed; fore and bottom
edges untrimmed.
Note: Poems. A combination reissue of the earlier *Irradiations Sand
and Spray* (1915) and *Goblins and Pagodas* (1916). Reprinted by
Macmillan in 1930; see I-A-6 and I-A-7 and I-A-13-a.

13-a. *Preludes and Symphonies*

PRELUDES AND / SYMPHONIES / BY / JOHN GOULD FLETCHER / NEW YORK / THE MACMILLAN COMPANY / 1930

   [A-K]⁸ [L]¹⁰ [i-viii] ix-xviii [1-2] 3-39 [40-42] 43-59 [60] [1-2] 3
[4] 5-9 [10] 11-15 [16] 17-20 [21-24] 25-29 [30] 31-37 [38] 39-44
[45] 46-51 [52] 53-60 [61] 62-65 [66] 67-73 [74] 75-80 [81] 82-85
[86] 87-91 [92] 93-98 [99-102]

   [i]: half-title; [ii]: publisher's device; [iii]: title; [iv]: copyright
page; [v]: dedication; [vi]: blank; [vii]: note; [viii]: blank; ix-xiv:
preface; xv-xviii: contents list; [1]-[60] [1]-[99] same as 1922
edition, see above; [100-102]: blank
Bound in blue cloth; cream label on spine with blue lettering.
Endpapers white. Top edges trimmed; fore and bottom edges
untrimmed.
Note: Poems. A reissue of the 1922 edition with a new preface
dated September 1929.

14. *Parables*

[title page within single rules] PARABLES / *By* /
JOHN GOULD FLETCHER / *with woodcut frontispiece* /
by / *John J. A. Murphy* / *LONDON* / *KEGAN
PAUL, TRENCH, TRUBNER & CO., LTD.* /
*BROADWAY HOUSE: 68-74 CARTER LANE,
E.C.* / *1925*

   [A]⁶ [1]⁸ 2-9⁸ [i-ii] [plate tipped in] [iii-iv] v-vii [viii] ix-xii
[1-4] 5-69 [70-74] 75-143 [144]

   [i]: half-title; [ii]: blank; [plate tipped in as frontispiece]; [iii]:
title; [iv]: colophon; v-vii: Prelude; [viii]: blank; ix-xii: contents
list; [1]: Book I. The Parable of Christ; [2]: dedication; [3]:

quotes; [4]: blank; 5-69: Parable (1921-1924); 5-6: I. 1919; 7-9: II. Battle-Song; 10-12: III. 1921; 13-14: IV. The Birth of Christ; 15-18: V. The Crucifixion [sic]; 18-19: VI. Immortality; 20-21: VII. To Almighty God; 22: VIII. To My Soul, or Yours; 23: IX. "Yea, a Sword shall pierce through thine own heart also"; 24-27: X. Fragments of Eternity; 27: XI. The Attainment; 28: XII. The Moment; 29-39: XIII. To the World; 31-32: XIV. To Europe; 33-34: XV. To Asia; 35: XVI. To America; 36: XVII. In Memoriam; 37: XVIII. Dewdrops; 38: XIX. The Word; 39-40: XX. The Path in the Night; 40: XXI. For Deliverance from Hell; 41: XXII. The Sending-Forth of the Apostles; 42-43: XXIII. The Everlasting Quest; 44: XXIV. To a Woman Clothed with the Sun; 45-46: XXV. The Mountain and the Butterfly; 47-49: XXVI. To a Starving Man; 48-49: XXVII. The Entombment; 50-51: XXVIII. The Last Judgment; 52: XXIX. Eden; 53: XXX. The End of the World; 54-55: XXI [sic]. The Procession; 56-57: XXXII. The Death of England; 57-58: XXXIII. The Gallery of Skulls; 59-60: XXXIV. The Secret of Mars; 61-62: XXXV. The New World; 63-64: XXXVI. The Way of Dust; 64-65: XXXVII. Christ and Antichrist; 66: XXXVIII. The Way of Christ; 67: XXXIX. The Fall of Antichrist; 68: XL. The Choice; 69: XLI. The Return Home; [70]: blank; [71]: Book II: The Parable of Antichrist; [72]: dedication; [73]: quotes; [74]: blank; 75-76: I. The New Beatitudes; 76: II. The Birth of Lucifer; 77: III. Against Immortality; 78-79: IV. After the Crucifixion [sic]; 80-82: V. The End of Job; 83: VI. The Second Prodigal Son; 84-85: VII. The Death of Prometheus; 86-87: VIII. The Levite and the Samaritan; 88-90: IX. The Burden of Ahasuerus; 91-93: X. Hard Sayings; 94: XI. On a Difference of Opinion; 95: XII. In Praise of Imperfection; 96-97: XIII. On a Moral Triumph; 98: XIV. On Ultimate Knowledge; 99: XV. The Buried Tent; 100-101: XVI. The Serpent's Wisdom; 102-103: XVII. The Judgment of the World; 104-106: XVIII. The Great Wall; 107-108: XIX. From a Sermon of Lucifer; 109: XX. The Dying Star; 110-111: XXI. To a Survivor of the Flood; 112-113: XXII. Battle-Song; 114-115: XXIII. The Blessing of the Worms; 116-117: XXIV. 1924; 118-119: XXV. The Death of God; 120: XXVI. On Progress; 121-122: XXVII. The Four Gods; 123: XXVIII. To the Christians; 124-125: XXIX. The Optimists and the Pessimist; 126-127: XXX. On Forgiveness; 128-131: XXXI. St. Francis and

the Rich Man; 132-134: XXXII. God and Mammon; 135-136:
XXXIII. The Last Farewell; 137-138: XXXIV. Buddhism and
Christianity; 139: XXXV. The Prayer of Antichrist; 140-141:
XXXVI. The New Genesis; 142-143: XXXVII. Towards
Olympus; [144]: blank
    Bound in black cloth; spine stamped in gold. Endpapers
white. All edges trimmed.
Note: Short prose poems. Expresses the view that man is left prey
to dualistic forces. The path to heaven is therefore in man
himself, and not in the dogma of religion.

15. *Branches of Adam*
     BRANCHES OF ADAM / By John Gould
     Fletcher / [printer's device] / LONDON / Faber and
     Gwyer [Copyright page:] First published in mcmxxvi
     . . .
         A-E⁸ F² [1-6] 7 [8] 9-10 [11-12] 13-31 [32] 33-47 [48] 49-67 [68]
     69-79 [80] 81 [82-84]
         [1-2]: blank; [3]: half-title; [4]: by the same author; [5]: title; [6]:
     First published in mcmxxvi by Faber and Gwyer Limited, 24
     Russell Square, London. Made and printed in Great Britain by the
     Westminster Press London; 7: dedication; [8]: blank; 9-10:
     preface; [11]: half-title; [12]: blank; 13-31: Book I; [32]: blank; 33-
     47: Book II; [48]: blank; 49-67: Book III; [68]: blank; 69-79: Book
     IV; [80]: blank; 81-[82]: Epilogue; [83]: blank; [84]: colophon
         Bound in brown cloth; cream label with black lettering on
     spine. Endpapers white. All edges untrimmed.
     Note: Poem. One long poem in four books plus epilogue.
     Originally was to be part of a still longer poem. The object of the
     poem is to show that good and evil coexist in the world, and that
     good in fact depends on evil and evil on good, and that it could not
     be otherwise. The premise which Fletcher draws from this is that
     chaos and disunion, not law and order, are the principles of life
     which sustain all things. Eighty-one copies were signed by the
     author.

16. *The Black Rock*

THE BLACK ROCK / *by* / John Gould Fletcher /
NEW YORK / THE MACMILLAN COMPANY /
1928

[A]⁸ B-M⁸ [i-vi] vii-xi [12-14] 15-64 [65-66] 67-118 [119-120]
121-144 [145-146] 147-164 [165-166] 167-187 [188-192]

[i]: half-title; [ii]: by the same author; [iii]: title; [iv]: Printed in
Great Britain; [v]: dedication; [vi]: acknowledgment; vii-xi:
contents lists; [12]: blank; [13]: Book I. Gateways; [14]: blank; 15-
17; Prelude: The Cloud; 18: The Last Frontier; 19: Dawn; 20-21:
At Sunrise; 22-23: The Cave; 24: Noon; 25: Repose; 26: An Hour;
27-28: Gates; 29-30: The Stone Place; 31: The Cliff-Wall; 32: The
Rain cloud; 33: The Day That Autumn Came; 34: The Burning
Mountain; 35-36: the Wanderer; 37-38: The Star; 39-40: Song of
the Watcher; 41: The Berry Picker; 42-43: The Tower; 44: The
Bridge; 45: The Swan; 46: Life; 47: You and I; 48: The Cataract;
49: The Arrival; 50: The Horizon; 51-53: Gulf Stream; 54: Sunset;
55: Twilight; 56: London Nightfall; 57: Exit; 58: The Home-
coming; 59: Blake; 60: Advent; 61: I Had Scarcely Fallen Asleep;
62: The Road; 63: Kingdoms; 64: Epilogue: Spring; [65]: Book II.
Dust Discrowned; [66]: blank; 67-68: Prelude: The Star Scatterer;
69: The Future; 70: Autumn; 71: The Enduring; 72: The Rock; 73:
Impromptu; 74: A Rebel; 75: Snowy Mountains; 76: Song of the
Mad Princess; 77-78: Song of the Old Man; 79-80: Song of
Progress; 81-82: Song of the Moderns; 83-84: Song of the Tower-
Builder; 85: The Portrait; 86-87: On My Own Face In the Glass;
88: Late Summer; 89: The Haunted House; 90: Sea-Violins; 91:
Crucifixion [*sic*] of the Skyscraper; 92: To a Nameless Child; 93:
Love Will Not Keep; 94-95: "Be Sure You Live In Vain: I Wish I
Had"; 96-97: Isle Iranim; 98: Sonnet; 99-100: The Lost Cause;
101-102: What the Public Wants; 103: Painted Women; 104: To
All Who Fail; 105: Epitaph On an Idealist; 106: Brahma; 107-108:
Buddha and Christ; 109: An Unbeliever to the Church; 110: On
One Who Died Young; 111: Whitman; 112-113: Second Advent;
114: The Stars; 115-116: Songs For One Dead; 117: Last
Judgment; 118: Envoi; [119]: Book III. The Black Rock; [120]:
blank; 121-130: Autobiography; 121-123: I. Before and After;
124-126: The River Flows; 126-127: The Ship Goes Down; 127-
130: That Which Was Left; 131-136: The Black Rock (To Thomas
Hardy); 137-141: Last Lines; 142-144: That Day; [145] Book IV.

Cycle of Liguria; [146]: blank; 147-152: To Columbus (To John J. A. Murphy); 153-154: The Olive; 155-156: The Cypress; 157-158: The Bell-Tower; 159-164: From Portofino Point (In Memoriam Friedrich Nietzsche); [165]: Book V. Prayer to the Unknown God; [166]: blank; 167-170: Hynm of Adam; 171-175: Prayers; 171: For the Wind; 171: For the Rain; 171-172: For Nakedness; 172: For Life; 172: For Death; 172-173: For Love; 173: For Wisdom; 173: For Conflict; 174: For Pity; 174: For Contempt; 174: For Renewal; 175: For Reconciliation; 176-[188]: To the Unknown God;[189-192]: blank

Bound in black cloth; spine has cream label with black lettering. Endpapers white. All edges trimmed.
Note: Poems. (See I-A-16-a.)

16.a.   *The Black Rock*

THE BLACK ROCK / *by* / John Gould Fletcher / LONDON / Faber & Gwyer [Copyright page:] [publisher's device] / FIRST PUBLISHED IN MCMXXVIII / BY FABER & GWYER LIMITED / 24 RUSSELL SQUARE LONDON W.C.I. / PRINTED IN GREAT BRITAIN / BY BUTLER & TANNER LIMITED / FROME AND LONDON

[A]⁸ B-M⁸ [i-vi] vii-xi [xii-xiv] 15-64 [65-66] 67-118 [119-120] 121-141 [145-146] 147-164 [165-166] 167-187 [188-192]

[i]: half-title; [ii]: by the same author; [iii]: title; [iv]: First published in MCMXXVIII by Faber & Gwyer Limited 24 Russell Square London W.C.I. Printed in Great Britain by Butler & Tanner Limited Frome and London.

Bound in black cloth; spine stamped in gold. Endpapers white. Top edges untrimmed; bottom and fore edges trimmed.
Note: Poems. Contents and pagination correspond exactly to I-A-16.

17.   *John Smith—Also Pocahontas*

[title page within double rules; title and author framed within single blue rules] John Smith- / *Also Pocahontas* / *By* JOHN GOULD FLETCHER / [ornament framed by single blue horizontal rules and double blue vertical rules] / [framed by single blue rules] NEW YORK [dot] BRENTANO'S [dot] PUBLISHER [Copyright page:] copyrighted 1928

[A]⁴[B-X]⁸ pp. [1-2] [i-v] v-vii [viii-xii] [1-2] 3-98 [plate] 99-128 [plate] 129-210 [plate] 211-270 [plate] 271-303 [304-306]

[pp. 1-2]: blank; [i]: half-title; [ii]: frontispiece portrait; [iii]: title; [iv]: copyright page; v-vii: introduction; [viii]: blank; [ix-x]: contents lists; [xi]: list of illustrations; [xii]: blank; [1]: half-title; [2]: quotes; 3-13: First Chapter: A Runaway Sets Out and Returns; 14-22: Second Chapter: He Goes Off to the Wars in High Hungary; 23-32: Third Chapter: He Wins a Coat of Arms from Three Turkish Champions before a Mythical City; 33-42: Fourth Chapter: On the Eternal Female, Turks, Tartars, and Traveller's Tales in General; 43-56: Fifth Chapter: Preparations for Virginia, together with Some Considerations on the Spirit of the Age; 57-71: Sixth Chapter: The Voyage and the Landfall; 72-83: Seventh Chapter: Trouble in Utopia; 84-96: Eighth Chapter: The Fall of Wingfield; 97-98 [plate: Pocahontas, The Daughter of King Powhatan] 99-106: Ninth Chapter: Powhatan and His People; 107-117: Tenth Chapter: The Red Man Hunts for Deer and Makes a Prisoner; 118-128 [plate: Pocahontas Pleading with King Powhatan to Spare Captain Smith's Life] 129-130: Eleventh Chapter: Powhatan Meets His Match; 131-144: Twelfth Chapter: The Arrival of Newport; 145-156: Thirteenth Chapter: Newport's Departure, Smith On the Warpath; 157-175: Fourteenth Chapter: The Discovery of the Chesapeake; 176-187: Fifteenth Chapter: Newport Fails at Last, Powhatan Shows His Hand; 188-201: Sixteenth Chapter: Things Move to a Crisis; 202-210 [plate: Captain John Smith Makes a Prisoner of the King of Pamaunkee] 211-219: Seventeenth Chapter: The Crisis and What Followed After; 220-230: Eighteenth Chapter: The White Men Win Every Battle, but Lose the War; 231-249: Nineteenth Chapter: The Fall of an Adventurer; 250-265: Twentieth Chapter: What Became of Pocahontas; 266-270 [plate: A Description of Part of the Adventures of Captain Smith in Virginia] 271-280: Twenty-first Chapter: Alarms and Excursions; 281-296: Twenty-second Chapter: Smith Makes the Landfall; 297-303: Bibliography; [304-306]: blank

Bound in blue cloth; spine and front stamped in gold. Endpapers white. Top edges trimmed; fore and bottom edges untrimmed.

Note: Historical biography. In Smith Fletcher saw a kindred spirit and fellow exile. The way in which Fletcher renders the Smith-Pocahontas legend serves to enhance the romantic reputation of Smith. (See I-A-17-a.)

17.a. *John Smith—Also Pocahontas*

[photographic reduction of 1928 title page within double rules; title and author framed within single rules]John Smith— / Also Pocahontas / By JOHN GOULD FLETCHER / [ornament framed by horizontal rules and double verticle rules] / [framed by single rules] NEW YORK [dot] BRENTANO'S [dot] PUBLISHER / [outside and beneath double rules] KRAUS REPRINT CO. / New York / 1972

[A-J]¹⁶ [K]⁴ [L]¹⁶ [i-iv] v-vii [viii-xii] [1-2]3-98 [plate] 99-128 [plate] 129-210 [plate] 211-270 [plate] 271-303 [304-308]

[i]: half-title; [ii]: frontispiece portrait; [iii]: title; [iv]: copyright page; v-vii: introduction; [viii]: blank; [ix-x]: contents list; [xi]: list of illustrations; [xii]:blank; [1]-303 same as I-A-17 above; [304-308]: blank

Bound in green buckram; spine stamped in gold. Endpapers white. All edges trimmed.

Note: Historical biography. Reprint of I-A-17.

18. *The Crisis of the Film*

[within double rules with ornament at each corner] The Crisis of / the Film / By / JOHN GOULD FLETCHER / [ornament] / 1929 / UNIVERSITY OF WASHINGTON BOOK STORE / SEATTLE

[A]²² [i-iv] [1-7] 8-35 [36-40]

[i-ii]: blank; [iii-iv]: University of Washington Chapbooks; [1]: half-title; [2]: blank; [3]: title; [4]: copyright page; [5]: half-title; [6]: blank; [7]-35: text; [36]: blank; [37]: See over leaf for advertisement of other publications; [38]: advertisement for chapbook no. 7; [39]: other publications; [40]: blank

Bound by staple at fold in red paper jacket with black lettering
and ornamentation over oaktag covers. All edges untrimmed.
Note: Essay. Fletcher forsees the artistic dominance of the
German film industry because of the tradition of Albrecht Dürer,
Hans Holbein, and Isaak Grünewald. He argues against the
innovation of the talkies. His view is that cinema is, or ought to
be, a symphony of pictures. This item is number 24 in the
University of Washington Chapbook Series, edited by Glenn
Hughes.

19. *The Two Frontiers: A Study In Historical Psychology*
[title, author, and imprint within maroon double
rules] THE TWO / FRONTIERS / A STUDY IN
HISTORICAL PSYCHOLOGY / [double maroon
horizontal rules] / JOHN GOULD
FLETCHER / PUBLISHED IN NEW YORK
BY / COWARD-McCANN, INC. / IN THE YEAR
1930

[A-Aa]⁸ [i-vi] [1-2] 3-102 [103-104] 105-187 [188-190] 191-290
[291-292] 293-373 [374] 375-377 [378]

[i]: half-title; [ii]: blank; [iii]: title; [iv]: copyright page; [v]:
dedication; [vi]: blank; [1]: Book I; [2]: quote; 3-24: Chapter I; 25-
46: Chapter II; 47-72: Chapter III; 73-102: Chapter IV; [103]:
Book II; [104]: quotes; 105-130: Chapter V; 131-147: Chapter VI;
148-163: Chapter VII; 164-187: Chapter VIII; [188]: blank; [189]:
Book III; [190]: quotes; 191-208: Chapter IX; 209-225: Chapter X;
226-246: Chapter XI; 247-266: Chapter XII; 267-290: Chapter
XIII; [291]: Book IV; [292]: quotes; 293-311: Chapter XIV; 312-
329: Chapter XV; 330-350: Chapter XVI; 351-373: Chapter XVII;
[374]: blank; 375-377: Bibliography; [378]: blank

Bound in maroon cloth; spine and front stamped in gold.
Endpapers yellow. Top edges trimmed; fore and bottom edges
untrimmed.
Note: Published in Europe with the title, *Europe's Two Frontiers: A
Study of the Historical Forces At Work in Russia and America As They Will
Increasingly Affect European Civilization*. (See I-A-20.)

20. *Europe's Two Frontiers*
    [title, author, and imprint within double rules]
    EUROPE'S / TWO FRONTIERS / *By* / JOHN
    GOULD FLETCHER / A Study of the
    historical / forces at work in Russia / and America as
    they will / increasingly affect European /
    civilization. / LONDON / EYRE & SPOTTISWOODE
    LIMITED / 1930

    [A+ A 1-2, B-Aa]⁸ [i-vi] [1-2] 3-102 [103-104] 105-187 [188-
    190] 191-290 [291-292] 293-373 [374] 375-377 [378]
    [i-ii]: blank; [iii]: title; [iv]: blank; [v]: dedication; [vi]: blank; [1]:
    Book I; [2]: quote; 3-24: Chapter I; 25-46: Chapter II; 47-72:
    Chapter III; 73-102: Chapter IV; [103]: Book II; [104]: quotes;
    105-130: Chapter V; 131-147: Chapter VI; 148-163: Chapter VII;
    164-187: Chapter VIII; [188]: blank; [189]: Book III; [190]: quotes;
    191-208: Chapter IX; 209-225: Chapter X; 226-246: Chapter XI;
    247-266: Chapter XII; 267-290: Chapter XIII; [291]: Book IV;
    [292]: quotes; 293-311: Chapter XIV; 312-329: Chapter XV; 330-
    350: Chapter XVI; 351-373: Chapter XVII; [374]: blank; 375-377:
    Bibliography; [378]: blank
    Bound in maroon cloth; spine stamped in gold. Endpapers dull
    gold. Top edges trimmed; fore and bottom edges untrimmed.
    Note: Published in the United States with the title *The Two Frontiers:
    A Study in Historical Psychology*. This edition is the American sheets
    with cancel title-leaf and conjugate flyleaf. See I-A-19.

21. *XXIV Elegies*
    JOHN GOULD FLETCHER / [in maroon] XXIV
    / [in maroon] ELEGIES / WRITER'S EDITIONS
    [dot] SANTA FE [dot] N [dot] M [dot] [Copyright
    page:] copyright 1935

    [A]⁶ [B-F]⁸ [G]⁶ [i-xii] 1-87 [88-92]
    [i-ii]: blank; [iii]: half-title; [iv]: "four hundred copies of *XXIV
    Elegies* have been printed by the Rydal Press for Writer's
    Editions each signed by the author John Gould Fletcher" [each
    copy is numbered and bears the author's signature]; [v]: title;
    [vi]: copyright page; [vii]: dedication; [viii]: blank; [ix]:
    acknowledgment; [x]: blank; [xi]: contents list; [xii]: blank; 1-3:

"Elegy on a Transatlantic Voyage"; 4-5: "Elegy on a Lost Ship";
6-8: "Elegy on the Jewish People"; 9-11: "Elegy for All Poets";
12-14: "Elegy on London"; 15-17: "Elegy in Cornwall"; 18-20:
"The Jade Elegy"; 21-23: "Elegy on Middle-Age"; 24-27: "Elegy
As Epithalamium"; 28-30: "Elegy on Two Edens"; 31-34: "Elegy
on Thomas Alva Edison"; 35-37: "Elegy on a Burnt Airship
(R101—October 1930)"; 38-40: "Elegy on the Building of the
Washington Bridge"; 41-44: "Elegy on an Empty Skyscraper";
45-50: "Elegy on the End of Love"; 51-54: "Elegy in a Civil War
Cemetery"; 55-57: "Elegy on a Nordic White Protestant"; 58-
62: "Elegy on a Gothic Cathedral"; 63-67: "Elegy on Napoleon
(My Name Means: the Lion of the Desert)"; 68-75: "Elegy on
the Russian Revolution"; 76-79: "Elegy on Tristan in Brittany";
80-82: "Elegy on Tintern Abbey (To Walter Edwin Peck)"; 83-
85: "Elegy on the Last Judgment"; 86-87: "Elegy for All the
Dead 1914-1918"; [88-92]: blank
    Bound in buff cloth; spine and front stamped in red.
Endpaper tan. Top and bottom edges trimmed, fore edges
untrimmed.
Note: Poems. Book published by Writer's Editions, a cooperative
group of writers living in the Southwest, who believed that
regional publication would foster the growth of American
literature. The poems are in the elegiac tradition,
the poet grieving over man's spiritual loss.

22. *Life Is My Song*
    [title, author, and imprint within double rules] Life Is
    My Song / [horizontal rule] / The Autobiography
    of / John Gould Fletcher / [horizontal rule] / Farrar
    & Rinehart / Incorporated / New York Toronto
    [copyright page:] copyright 1937
        [A-N]¹⁶ [i-vi] [1-2] 3-395 [396] [397-406] [407-410]
        [i]: half-title; [ii]: books by John Gould Fletcher; [iii]: title; [iv]:
    copyright page; [v]: dedication; [vi]: blank; [1]: Life Is My Song
    The Autobiography of John Gould Fletcher; [2]: blank; 3-395:
    text; [396]: blank; 397-406: index; [407-410]: blank
        Bound in green cloth; spine and front stamped in black.
    Variant copy bound in red cloth; stamped in gold on spine and
    front; top edges yellow. Endpapers white. All edges trimmed.
    Note: Autobiography.

23. *Selected Poems*

SELECTED / POEMS / *by* / JOHN GOULD
FLETCHER / [ornament] / FARRAR &
RINEHART, INC. / NEW YORK TORONTO
[Copyright page:]copyright 1938

[A-Q]⁸ [i-viii] ix-xii [1-2] 3-38 [39-40] 42-65 [66-68] 69-
103 [104-106] 107-129 [130-132] 133-162 [163-164] 165-216
[217-218] 219-237 [238-244]

[i]: half-title; [ii]: books by John Gould Fletcher; [iii]: title; [iv]:
copyright page; [v]: dedication; [vi]: blank; [vii]: acknowledg-
ment; [viii]: blank; ix-xii: contents lists; [1]: Part One; [2]:
blank; 3-10: Irradiations; 3: I; 4: II; 4-5: III; 5: IV; 6: V, VI; 7:
VII; 7-8: VIII; 8: IX; 8-9: X; 9: XI; 9-10: XII; 10-15: Sand and
Spray; 10-11: The Gale; 12: The Tide; 13: Steamers; 14: The
Night Wind; 14-15: Tide of Storms; 15-19: Blue Symphony;
20-25: Green Symphony; 25-32: White Symphony; 32-38:
Poppies of the Red Year: A Symphony in Scarlet; [39]: Part
Two; [40]: blank; 41-42: The Walk on the Beach; 42-44: The
Walk in the Garden; 44-45: The Aster FLower; 45-47:
Autumnal Clouds; 47: Faith; 48-49: Reunion; 49-50: On the
Beach; 50-52: On the Verandah; 52-53: In the Garden of
Dreams; 54-55: The Offering; 55-61: The Empty Days; 61-63:
In Memory of a Night; 64-65: Epilogue; [66]: blank; [67]: Part
Three; [68]: blank; 69-74: Clipper Ships; 74-78: Down the
Mississippi; 74-75: Embarkation; 75: Heat; 75-76: Full Moon;
76: The Moon's Orchestra; 77: The Stevedores; 77-78: Night
Landing; 78: The Silence; 78-83: The Old South; 83-87: The
Passing of the South; 87-90: In the City of Night (To the
Memory of Edgar Allan Poe); 90-95: Arizona Poems; 90-91:
The Well in the Desert; 91-93: Mexican Quarter; 93-94: Cliff-
Dwelling; 94-95: The Windmills; 95-99: The Grand Canyon of
the Colorado; 99-103: Lincoln; [104]: blank; [105]: Part Four;
[106]: blank; 107-108: The Last Frontier; 108: The Swan; 109:
The Cataract; 109-111: Gulf Stream; 111-112: Sunset; 112-113:
Exit; 113: Blake; 114: Advent; 114-115: I Had Scarcely Fallen
Asleep; 115: Spring; 116: The Future; 117: Autumn; 117-118:
The Enduring; 118-119: The Rock; 119-120: Song of the
Moderns; 120-121: The Portrait; 121-122: Late Summer; 122-
123: Crucifixion [*sic*] of the Skyscraper; 123-124: Isle Iranim;
124-125: Buddha and Christ; 126: An Unbeliever to the

Church; 127: Whitman; 127-128: Songs for One Dead; 129:
Last Judgment; [130]: blank; [131]: Part Five; [132]: blank; 133-
142: Autobiography; 133-135: Before and After; 136-138: The
River Flows; 138-139: The Ship Goes Down; 139-142: That
Which Was Left; 142-148: The Black Rock (To Thomas Hardy);
148-150: That Day; 150-155: To Columbus; 156-157: The
Olive; 157-162: From Portofino Point (In Memoriam Friedrich
Nietzśche); [163]: Part Six; [164]: blank; 165-168: Elegy on a
Transatlantic Voyage; 168-171: Elegy on the Jewish People;
171-175: Elegy on London; 175-178: The Jade Elegy; 178-182:
Elegy as Epithalamium; 183-187: Elegy on Thomas Alva Edison;
187-190: Elegy on the Building of the Washington Bridge; 190-
194: Elegy on an Empty Skyscraper; 194-200: Elegy on
Napoleon: 200-208: Elegy on the Russian Revolution; 208-211:
Elegy on Tintern Abbey; 211-214: Elegy on the Last Judgment;
214-216: Elegy For All the Dead; [217]: Part Seven; [218]:
blank; 219-220: The Prelude of Storm; 220: Song of the
Midnight Rain; 221: Promenade By the Autumn River; 222-
223: Rhapsody of Indian Summer; 223-224: The Gifts
Demanded; 224: To an Autumn Rose; 225: The Vow; 225-228:
Conversation with a Midwinter Sky; 228-229: To a Face in the
Firelight; 229-233: Symphony of the New Year; 234-235: At
the Old House; 235-237: Ascent of Monadnock; [238-244]:
blank

   Bound in maroon cloth; spine stamped in silver; front
stamped with the author's signature. Endpapers white. Top
and bottom edges trimmed; top edges stained red; fore edges
untrimmed.
   Note: Poems. Winner of the 1938 Pulitzer Prize for poetry. A
collection of what the author considers to be his best poems to
date.

24. *South Star*

   SOUTH STAR / BY / JOHN GOULD
   FLETCHER / NEW YORK / THE MACMILLAN
   COMPANY / 1941
      [A-H]⁸ [i-x] [1-2] 3-50 [51-52] 53-88 [89-90] 91-97 [98-100]
   101-112 [113-114] 115-117 [118]
      [i]: half-title; [ii]: printer's device; [iii]: title; [iv]: copyright
   page; [v]: dedication; [vi]: blank; [vii]: note; [viii]: blank; [ix]:

contents list; [x]: blank; [1]: I. The Story of Arkansas; [2]:
blank; 3-13: Book I. De Soto Discovers Arkansas; 14-25: Book
II. France Founds Arkansas; 26-40: Book III. The Pioneers in
Arkansas; 41-50: Book IV. Arkansas Faces Its Future; [51]: II.
Echoes of Arkansas; [52]: blank; 53: My Father's Watch; 54-57:
In Mount Holly (J.G.F. and A. K.F., 1906-1910); 58-60:
Magnolia; 61: Christmas Tree; 62: The Scythe; 63: The
Journey; 64: By Old River; 65-66: The Unfamiliar House; 67-
70: The Pioneers; 71-72: Lost Corner; 73-75: On My Father's
Hundredth Birthday (6 January 1831-6 January 1931); 76-78:
Grandfather's Grave; 79-81: Conversation With an Important
Ghost; 82-83: Arkansas Red Haw; 84-86: The Three Oaks; 87-
88: The Farewell; [89]: III. Upper South; [90]: blank; 91:
Dogwood; 92: The Fireflies; 93-94: Thunderstorm in the
Ozarks; 95: Summer Dusk; 96-97: Hillbilly Philosophy; [98]:
blank; [99]: IV. Deep South; [100]: blank; 101-103: Big River;
104-105: The House to the Man; 106-107: Liveoak and
Parasite; 108: South Wind; 109-110: The Song of Liveoak Hill;
111-112: The Song of Natchez Under the Hill; [113]: Epilogue;
[114]: blank; 115-116: Towards the North Star; 117:
acknowledgment; [118]: blank

    Bound in blue cloth; spine and front lettered in white.
Endpapers blue. All edges trimmed.

Note: Prose and poems. The first four books are historical prose
treatment of Arkansas. Underlying the short lyric poems which
are about Arkansas and other Southern subjects, is an attitude of
anti-industrialization and primitivist philosophy.

25. *The Burning Mountain*

    [title and author within a frame of triple rules with
silhouette of mountain at bottom] The Bur-
ning / Mountain / John Gould / Fletcher / *New
York* / E P DUTTON & COMPANY INC / 1946

     [A-F]⁸ [1-10] 11-96

     [1]: half-title; [2]: also by John Gould Fletcher; [3]: title; [4]:
copyright page; [5]: dedication; [6]: blank; [7]: contents list; [8]:
acknowledgment; [9]: half-title; [10]: blank; 11-12: Shadow on
the Prairie; 13-16: On Mesa Verde; 17-18: Requiem for a
Twentieth-Century Outlaw (In Memoriam, Charles, "Pretty
Boy," Floyd); 19-22: Ode to New York; 23-26: Symphony of

Snow; 27-29: The Flood Symphony; 30-33: Spain, 1936-39;
34-36: The Burning Mountain (A Legend of the Santa Fé
Trail); 37-38: The Ozarks; 39-40: Memorial for Summer, 1940;
41-46: August, 1940; 47-51: The Fallen Woods (New England
Hurricane, Sept. 21, 1939—Fall of France, 1940); 52-56: Good
Friday; 57-62: Journey Day (To Charlie May); 63-64: Salem
Campground; 65-68: The Land Is Cleared; 69-71: The Statue of
Liberty Speaks. 1941 (Dedicated October 28, 1886, by
President Grover Cleveland); 72-75: The Tiger's Hour; 76-78:
Long Journey, Late Arrival; 79-83: Repose in Strife; 84-87: The
Pioneer Year; 88-91: The Builders of the Bridge (In Memoriam
James Franklin Lewis); 92-93: The First Lot (Summer, 1941);
94-96: To the Twentieth Century (To Scott Greer)

   Bound in lavender cloth; spine stamped in gold; front
stamped in gold within frame of stamped double rules.
Endpapers white. Top and bottom edges trimmed; fore edges
untrimmed.

Note: Poems. Verso of title page states that twenty-five hundred
copies of the first edition have been printed. The title is derived
from a legend of the Santa Fé trail—a symbolic mountain which
served as a landmark to pioneers. The volume is strongly flavored
with the teaching of Taoism.

26. *Arkansas*

   [double rule] / *Arkansas* / [double rule] / JOHN
   GOULD FLETCHER / *Chapel Hill* / THE UNIVER-
   SITY OF NORTH CAROLINA PRESS / 1947

      [A-Dd]8 [i-viii] ix-x [1-3] 4-9 [10] 11-25 [26] 27-37 [38] 39-57
   [58] 59-76 [77] 78-89 [90] 91-107 [108] 109-130 [131] 132-143
   [144] 145-152 [153] 154-172 [173] 174-196 [197] 198-222 [223]
   224-235 [236] 237-264 [265] 266-286 [287] 288-301 [302] 303-
   314 [315] 316-334 [335] 336-353 [354] 355-365 [366] 367-383
   [384] 385-401 [402-403] 404-405 [406] 407-421 [422]

      [i]: half-title; [ii]: blank; [iii]: title; [iv]: copyright page; [v]:
   dedication; [vi]: blank; [vii]: note to the reader; [viii]: blank; ix-
   x: contents list; [1]: half-title; [2]: blank; [3]-9: One. A Look
   Around the Land; [10]-25: Two. A Spaniard Comes to See the
   Land and Does Not Depart; [26]-37: Three. The French Make a
   Map and Leave Behind Some Names; [38]-57: Four. A Traveller
   Sees Arkansas Become a Territory; [58]-76: Five. Pistols for

Bound in tan cloth with brown lettering and ornamentation on spine. Endpapers white with map of Arkansas and historical drawings in brown. All edges trimmed, top edges stained red. *Note*: History. Considered by many to be the finest history yet written about his native state. Interprets the state's history primarily from an economic perspective. Concludes that the racial issue serves only as a smoke screen for the state's economy being controlled by vested interests, both foreign and domestic.

B. Articles, Poems, and Reviews

1. Fletcher, John Gould. "Irradiations."
    Poetry, 3 (December 1913), 85-91.

    Poem. His first American publication. An indication that he
    had developed a distinctive style of his own. Reprinted in
    Irradiations, Sand and Spray (1915), *Preludes and Symphonies* (1922 and
    1930), and *Selected Poems* (1938). See I-A-6, I-A-13, and I-A-23.

2. ———. "Poems: A Selection from 'Irradiations.' " *Egoist*,
    1 (2 March 1914), 89-90.

    Poem. Includes parts 1, 2, 8, 9, 30, 32, 34, and Epilogue of the
    larger work. See I-A-6.

3. ———. "Cherokee Ballads." *Poetry and Drama*, 2 (June
    1914), 144-49.

    Poems. Includes: 1. "The Thunderstorm"; 2. "In the Tent"; 3.
    "Beyond the Campfire"; 4. "The Dotard"; 5. "Wounded"; 6.
    "Retreat"; 7. "The Duel"; 8. "After" (Reprinted in *The Tree of
    Life*); 9. "War-Song" (Reprinted in *Breakers and Granite*); and 10.
    "Song of Victory". See I-A-9 and I-A-11.

4. ———. "Poems." *Egoist*, 1 (1 June 1914), 211-12.
    Poems. Numbered 1-8, untitled.

5. ———. "Poems: London Excursion II." *Egoist*, 1 (15 July
    1914), 275-76.

    Poems. Includes "Bus," "Approach," "Arrival" (c.f. "The
    Arrival," *The Black Rock*, p. 49), "Walk," "Bus-top," "Transpor-
    tation," "Peripeteia," "Mid-flight," and "Station."

6. ———. "Blue Symphony." *Poetry*, 4 (September 1914),
    211-15.

    Poem. As with his other color symphonies, this is an attempt
    to describe mood in terms of the senses. Reprinted in *Goblins
    and Pagodas* (1916), *Preludes and Symphonies* (1922 and 1930), and
    Selected Poems (1938). See I-A-7, I-A-13, and I-A-23.

7. ———. "Magazitis Americana—A Diagnosis." *Smart Set*,
   44 (September 1914), 47-49.
   Poem.

8. ———. "War Poetry" and "Orange Symphony." *Egoist*,
   1 (2 November 1914), 410-12.
   Poems. "War Poetry" is a prose poem. "Orange Symphony"
   is reprinted in *Goblins and Pagodas* (1916) and *Preludes and
   Symphonies* (1922 and 1930). See I-A-7, I-A-13.

9. ———. "More War Poetry." *Egoist*, 1 (16 November
   1914), 424-46.
   Essay (almost a prose poem). Quotes poetry of the past in
   the context of the present World War.

10. ———. "Green Symphony." *Little Review*, 1 (February
    1915), 14-17.
    Poem. Reprinted in *Goblins and Pagodas* (1916), *Preludes and
    Symphonies* (1922 and 1930), and *Selected Poems* (1938), also in *Book
    Notes Illustrated*, (5 April-May 1927), p. 135. See I-A-7, I-A-13,
    and I-A-23.

11. ———. "Miss Lowell's Discovery: Polyphonic Prose."
    Poetry, 6 (April 1915), 32-36.
    Essay. Focuses on Any Lowell's technique of combining
    recitives of *vers libre* with fast flowing metrical lines linked by
    connecting passages of prose, while employing orchestration of
    sound by means of assonance, alliteration, and repetition.

12. ———. "Vers Libre and Advertisements." *Little Review*,
    2 (April 1915), 29-30.
    Essay. A satirical comment achieved by juxtaposing some
    contemporary ad writing against contemporary poetry—
    "Gentlemen of the poet's profession, be ashamed of
    yourselves!"

13. ———. "America, 1915." *Little Review*, 2 (May 1915),
    23-25.
    Essay. A strange surreal depiction of the America from
    which Fletcher sees himself as having escaped.

14. ———. "Chicago." *Egoist*, 2 (1 May 1915), 74-75.

    Prose poem. Dedicated "to Harriet Monroe who founded Imagism."

15. ———. "The Poetry of Amy Lowell." *Egoist*, 2 (1 May 1915), 81-82.

    Essay. Provides good insight into the process by which images are distilled "into cameos."

16. ———. "The Old South" and "New York." *Poetry*, 6 (July 1915), 181-87.

    Poems. "The Old South" is reprinted in *Breakers and Granite* (1921) and *Selected Poems* (1938). "New York" is reprinted in *Breakers and Granite* (1921). See I-A-11 and I-A-23.

17. ———. "The Poet." *Poetry Journal*, 3 (July 1915), 231.

    Poem. Cf. "The Poet, I" and "The Poet, II", *Fire and Wine* (1913). See I-A-3.

18. ———. "Japanese Prints." *Egoist*, 2 (2 August 1915), 126.

    Poems. Reprinted in *Japanese Prints* (1918). See I-A-8.

19. ———. "Clipper Ships." *New Republic*, 4 (14 August 1915), 42-43.

    Poem. Reprinted in *Breakers and Granite* (1921) and *Selected Poems* (1938). See I-A-11, I-A-23; see also I-D-11 and I-D-12.

20. ———. "The Ghost of an Old House." *Egoist*, 3 (1 September 1915), 143.

    Poem. Comprised of "Prologue," "Bedroom," "Library," and "Indian Skull." Continued in *Egoist* (1 October 1915) and (1 November 1915); see I-B-22 and I-B-23. Reprinted in *Goblins and Pagodas* (1916) and *Preludes and Symphonies* (1922 and 1930). See I-A-7, I-A-13; see also *Current Opinion*, 61 (July 1916), p. 54.

21. ———. "Songs of Arkansas." *Others: A Magazine of the New Verse*, No. 3 (1915), 41-49.

    Poem. Includes "Invocation," "Women's Song at the Time of

the Green-Corn Dance," and "War Song." Reprinted in *Breakers and Granite* (1921). See I-A-11.

22. ———. "Ghosts of an Old House." *Egoist*, 2 (1 October 1915), 157-58.

Poem. Comprised of "Old Nursery," "Now My Bedroom," "Attic," "The Calendar in the Attic," "The Hoopskirt," "The Yardstick," "The Little Chair," "In the Dark Corner," "The Three Oaks," "An Oak," and "Another Oak." Continued from *Egoist* (1 September 1915); see I-B-20. Continued in *Egoist* (1 November 1915); see I-B-23. See I-A-7, I-A-13; see also *Current Opinion*, 61 (July 1916), p. 54.

23. ———. "Ghosts of an Old House (continued)." *Egoist*, 2 (1 November 1915), 177-78.

Poem. Comprised of "The Backstairs," "The Cellar," "The Old Barn," "The Wall Cabinet," "The Trees," "The Well," "The Front Door," "The Toy Cabinet," "Vision," and "Epilogue." There is also a woodcut of Fletcher by Raoul Kristian. Continued from *Egoist* (1 September 1915) and (1 October 1915); see I-B-20 and I-B-22. Reprinted in *Goblins and Pagodas* (1915) and *Preludes and Symphonies* (1922 and 1930). See I-A-7, I-A-13; see also *Current Opinion*, 61 (July 1916), p. 54.

24. ———. "A Poet's Declaration of Rights." *Poetry*, 7 (November 1915), 88-89.

Essay. The right to work, think, experience and to create— the poet has the right to these four lives and must fight for them.

25. ———. "The Blue Symphony" and "London Excursion." *Some Imagist Poets, 1915: An Annual Anthology*. Boston: Houghton Mifflin, 1915, pp. 33-49.

Poems. "The Blue Symphony" was originally published in *Poetry* (September 1914); see I-B-6. "London Excursion" was originally published in *Egoist* (15 July 1914); see I-B-5.

26. ———. "Poppies of the Red Year." *New Republic*, 5 (15 January 1916), 280-81.

Poem. Reprinted as "Poppies of the Red Year: A Symphony in Scarlet," in *Goblins and Pagodas* (1916) and *Preludes and Symphonies* (1922 and 1930) and in *Selected Poems* (1938). See I-A-7, I-A-13, and I-A-23.

27. ———. "The Song of the Wind." *The Trimmed Lamp*, 5 (February 1916), 143.

Prose poem. Reprinted in *Breakers and Granite* (1921). See I-A-11.

28. ———. "Power-Station," "Shadows," and "The Spring Piper." *Poetry Journal*, 5 (March 1916), 60-63.

Poems. Reprinted in *Current Opinion* (May 1916), p. 353.

29. ———. "Patterns in Criticism." *Reedy's Mirror*, 25 (4 February 1916), 74-75.

Letter. [unverified].

30. ———. "Arizona Poems." *Poetry*, 7 (March 1916), 271-76.

Poems. Comprised of "The Well in the Desert," "Mexican Quarter," "Cliff Dwelling," and "Rain in the Desert." Reprinted in *Breakers and Granite* (1921) and *Selected Poems* (1938). Other short poems will later be added to these under the title "Arizona Poems." See I-A-11 and I-A-23.

31. ———. "Rupert Brooke: An Estimate." *The Trimmed Lamp*, 5 (March 1916), 157-59.

Essay. Weighs the importance of the artist's attitude towards his work against the achievement of the work itself.

32. ———. "Clover Leaf Culture." Rev. of *My Marjonary* by Robert Carlton Brown. *Poetry Journal*, 5 (April 1916), 121-24.

Fletcher's readiness to critically accept innovative verse is noteworthy.

33. ———. "A Puritan Artist: John Singer Sargent." *The Trimmed Lamp*, 5 (April 1916), 177-78.

    Essay. Views Sargent's art as an expression of the Puritan temperament at its apogee. Suggests that failures as an artist are linked to the venturing into decorative painting instead of remaining satisfied with his landscapes and portraits.

34. ———. "Mr. Aldington's Images." Rev. of *Images Old and New* by Richard Aldington. *Poetry*, 8 (April 1916), 49-51.

    Notes that recently there have been signs in England of a "return to simplicity and restraint which are the highest quality of art . . ." Sees American poetry as an "incohate vastness . . . material and of . . . intertangled racial current . . . haphazardness of methods and institutions, all [driving us] towards a poetry which is ephemeral in that it is hectic, disorganized, lacking in reflective judgment."

35. ———. "Three Imagist Poets." *Little Review*, 3 (May 1916), 30-35.

    Essay. Fletcher cites what he considers to be the four cardinal principles of the Imagist movement. The "three Imagist poets" are Richard Aldington, H. D., and F. S. Flint. Aldington is the only one discussed here; Flint and H.D. are discussed in a continuation of this article in *Little Review* (June-July 1916). See I-B-38.

36. ———. "Budding Imagists and Others." Rev. of *Others; An Anthology of New Verse*, ed. Alfred Kreymborg. *Poetry Journal*, 6 (June 1916), 157-63.

    Fletcher's disparaging remarks about Carl Sandburg, William Carlos Williams, Wallace Stevens, T. S. Eliot, all who will surpass him in reputation, are ironic, as well as interesting.

37. ———. "Spring." *Poetry Review of America*, June 1916, p. 8.

    Poem. Reprinted in *Selected Poems* (1938). Also see *The Black Rock* (1928). See I-A-23 and I-A-16.

38. ———. "Three Imagist Poets: II." *Little Review*, 3 (June-July 1916), 32-41.

> Essay. A discussion of F. S. Flint and H. D. Continued from *Little Review* (May 1916). See I-B-35.

39. ———. "Broadway's Canyon." *Craftsman*, 30 (July 1916), 364.

> Poem. Reprinted in *Breakers and Granite* (1921). See I-A-11.

40. ———. "Dirge of the Work-Horses." *Others: A Magazine of the New Verse*, 3 (July 1916), 11.

> Poem.

41. ———. "A Poet of Illusions." Rev. of *Turns and Movies* by Conrad Aiken. *Poetry Journal*, 6 (July 1916), 24-26.

> Fletcher's comment in defense of Aiken's craftsmanship is, "I have never heard that the muse is a cow-girl, with a skinny neck and long shoulder-blades, or that the Greeks left their statues unpolished."

42. ———. "Lincoln." *Poetry Review of America*, August 1916, p. 56.

> Poem. Reprinted in *Breakers and Granite* (1921) and *Selected Poems* (1938); also reprinted in *Current Opinion* (October 1916), p. 269 and in *Some Imagist Poets, 1917*. See I-A-II, I-A-23, I-B-64, and I-D-8.

43. ———. "Sologub's Created Legend." Rev. of *The Created Legend* by Feodor Sologub, tr. John Cournos. *Egoist*, 3 (November 1916), 167-68.

> Interesting not only for Fletcher's views on Russian literature but for the revelation, "Russia is the land of survivals of the past." The events of 1917 were evidently not anticipated by Fletcher.

44. ———. "Amores." Rev. of *Amores* by D. H. Lawrence. *Egoist*, 3 (December 1916), 182.

> Views Lawrence's artistic plight in the English environment. ". . . had this man been born in France he might have been another Baudelaire."

45. ———. "Flashes of Lightning." Rev. of *Flashlights* by
    Mary Aldis. *Poetry Journal*, 6 (December 1916), 71-75.

   It is not often, Fletcher notes, that one finds a woman poet who
   deliberately eschews the sentimental lyric for the stark. Finds this
   book somewhat more than mere realism, helped by its sense of
   dignity and beauty of suffering even under the most outwardly
   sordid forms and circumstances.

46. ———. "The March of the Dead Men." *Poetry Journal*, 6
    (December 1916), 41-42.

   Poem.

47. ———. "Last Rally." *Century*, 93 (December 1916), [297].

   Poem.

48. ———. "Modern Lamentation." *Poetry*, 9 (December
    1916), 137-40.

   Poem. Comprised of "Give and Take," "The Everlasting
   Contradiction" (c.f. "The Everlasting Paradox", *Visions of the
   Evening* (1913), I-A-5), "Blind People," and "Why the War."

49. ———. "On Subject Matter and War Poetry." *Egoist*, 3
    (December 1916), 188-89.

   Essay. States that no artist creates his subject matter, but is,
   rather, affected by it. A defense of Imagism's affinity for the
   mundane.

50. ———. "Arizona," "The Unquiet Street," "In the
    Theatre," "Ships in the Harbour," "The Empty
    House," and "The Skaters." *Some Imagist Poets, 1916: An
    Annual Anthology*. Boston: Houghton Mifflin, 1916, pp.
    35-48.

   Poems. See "Arizona" with "Arizona Poems," *Poetry* (March
   1916). See I-B-30. Reprinted in *Breakers and Granite* (1921) and
   Selected Poems (1938). "The Empty House" is reprinted in *The Tree of
   Life* (1918). See also I-A-11, I-A-23, and I-A-9.

51. ———. "Secret of Far Eastern Painting." *Dial*, 62 (11 January 1917), 3-7.

Essay. States that "a true education is that which trains the senses to investigate for themselves, the brain to correlate sensation, the spirit to receive it and give it out to the world." Makes point that it is necessary to not create the whole object but rather to focus on one aspect which will contain all the emotional impact. Style, Fletcher expounds, "is the universal morality of art." This essay provides only a cursory study of oriental art, but is extremely valuable in that it reveals the effect which it has had on Fletcher's art.

52. ———. "H. D.'s Vision." Rev. of *Sea-garden* by H. D. *Poetry*, 9 (February 1917), 266-69.

Theorizes that in order to appreciate H. D.'s poetry one must read it with a receptive mind—as one must all mystics.

53. ———. "A Misleading Anthology." Rev. of *Anthology of Magazine Verse for 1916*, edited by William Stanley Braithwaite. *Poetry Journal*, 6 (February 1917), 170-76.

Takes issue with Braithwaite's perception of the current poetry scene, by way of providing his own perception of the various movements and schools current.

54. ———. "Near Yarmouth" and "Rooms." *Bookman*, 45 (March 1917), 32-33.

Poems.

55. ———. "Yale Discovers Blake." Rev. of *Selections from the Symbolical Poems of William Blake* by Fred E. Pierce. *Poetry*, 9 (March 1917), 315-20.

Asserts that Blake's recognition as a poet has been slow in arriving because he is too much of the spiritual aristocrat for America. There is an interesting discussion of the importance of Blake's *Vala* and of Blake's supposed madness.

56. ———. "The Death of the Machines." *Egoist*, 3 (April 1917), 45-46.

  Essay. Looks at art as an anomaly against the backdrop of the war.

57. ———. "Japanese Prints." *Poetry Journal*, 7 (June 1917), 81-86.

  Poems. Includes "The Clouds" (c.f. "The Clouds," *The Dominant City* [1913], I-A-2 and "Clouds," *Visions of the Evening* [1913], I-A-2 and "Clouds," *Visions of the Evening* [1913], I-A-5), "Two Ladies Contrasted," "Distant Coasts," "On the Banks of the Sumida," "Yoshiwara Festival," "Sharaku Dreams," "The Beautiful Geisha," "Dead Thoughts," "A Comparison," "Mutability," "Despair," and "The Lonely Grave." All are reprinted in *Japanese Prints* (1918). See I-A-8. See also "Japanese Prints," *Egoist* (2 August 1915), I-B-18.

58. ———. "Living History." *Poetry*, 10 (June 1917), 149-53.

  Editorial comment. Sees America as "explosive with energy, but finds no outlet for that energy." American literature is becoming vulgar, a heritage of the people, rather than a plaything of the cultivated—presents Amy Lowell's *Men, Women, and Ghosts* and *Bronze Tablets* as an example of this.

59. ———. "Poetry of Ralph Hodgson." *Dial*, 63 (19 July 1917), 50-52.

  A quasi-review of Hodgson's book of poetry. Fletcher faults American poetry as exhibiting the obvious faults of the nation which has not yet hammered out its own literary tradition.

60. ———. "Heat." *Lyric*, 1 (August 1917), 5.

  Poem.

61. ———. "Night on the Beach." *Dial*, 63 (22 November 1917), 525.

  Poem.

62. ———. "Chicago Notes" and "War Angles." *Poetry*, 11 (December 1917), 139-43.

  Poems. "Chicago Notes" is comprised of "Lake Front at Night" (c.f. "Lake Shore at Night" in *Breakers and Granite* [1921], I-A-11) and, "The Monadnock" (c.f. "Ascent of Monadnock" in *Selected Poems* (1938), I-A-23, and "LaSalle Street—Evening").

63. ———. "Snow." *Lyric*, 2 (December 1917), 14-15.
   Poem. Reprinted in *Literary Digest*, 19 January 1918, p. 38.

64. ———. "Lincoln," "Blackberry-Harvest," "Moonlight," "Dawn," and "Armies." *Some Imagist Poets, 1917 An Annual Anthology*. Boston: Houghton Mifflin, 1917. pp. 39-52.
   Poems. "Lincoln" originally published in *Poetry Review of America* (August 1916), p. 56 and is reprinted in *Breakers and Granite* (1921), I-A-11 and *Selected Poems* (1938), I-A-23. See I-B-42. See also "Dawn" in, *The Dominant City* (1913), I-A-2.

65. ———. "Channel Sunset." *New Republic*, 13 (5 January 1918), 276.
   Poem.

66. ———. "The Great Silence: To Richard Aldington." *Poetry Journal*, 8 (January 1918), 50-52.
   Poem. Reprinted in *Current Opinion*, 64 (May 1918), p. 355.

67. ———. "Earth." *Bookman*, 47 (March 1918), [92].
   Poem.

68. ———. "Harold Monro." *Poetry Journal*, 8 (March 1918), 107-15.
   Essay. Sees British poetry as having been unable to develop for the past fifteen years. Suggests that Monro will probably be classed with the poets who might have been but weren't. There is irony in Fletcher's conclusion, because critics have levelled the same judgment at him.

69. ———. "The New God." *Egoist*, 5 (March 1918), 45-46.
   Essay. The tank enters the lexicon with the impact of a new god.

70. ———. "The Poetry of Conrad Aiken." Rev. of *Nocturne of Remembered Spring and Other Poems* by Conrad Aiken. *Dial*, 64 (28 March 1918), 291-92.

   The poet must constantly employ not only his mind, but his feelings as well. He must see the world not only as objective phenomena for meditation, but as subjective influence for emotion.

71. ———. "A New Heaven A Poem." *Yale Review*, 7 (April 1918), [527]-28.

   Poem. Reprinted in *Current Opinion*, 64 (June 1918), p. 427.

72. ———. "Russia." *Poetry*, 12 (April 1918), 22-29.

   Poem. Six months following the revolution, this poem bears particular import in that one can see how deeply Fletcher was impressed by the cataclysmic events taking place in the newly formed Soviet Union. Russia will be a continuing interest for Fletcher.

73. ———. "Two American Poets." Rev. of *Nocturne of Remembered Spring and Other Poems* by Conrad Aiken and *Al Que Quiere!* by William Carlos Williams. *Egoist*, 5 (April 1918), 60.

   Fletcher states his esteem for both writers.

74. ———. "Hard and Soft." *Poetry*, 12 (May 1918), 111-12.

   Letter to editor. Takes issue with some of Ezra Pound's comments in "The Hard and Soft in French Poetry," *Poetry* (February 1918). Fletcher sees two kinds of poetical emotion, the musical and the pictorial, upon which he elaborates.

75. ———. "Thomas Hardy's Poetry." Rev. of *Moments of Vision* by Thomas Hardy. *Poetry*, 12 (May 1918), 96-101.

   Considers Hardy to be the greatest living English poet. Suggests that Hardy ought not be considered in the context of English literature, since this would destroy his work of the last twenty years. After Robert Browning, Algernon Charles Swinburne, and Alfred Tennyson passed from the scene, only

George Meredith and Hardy possessed vitality. Of particular
interest are Fletcher's comments regarding what he views as a
strain of atavism running through Hardy's work.

76. ———. "London: A War Nocturne." *Dial*, 64 (11 July
1918), 53.
>   Poem.

77. ———. "A Modern Evangelist." Rev. of *Look! We Have
Come Through!* by D. H. Lawrence. *Poetry*, 12 (August
1918), 269-74.
>   Chides the English press for ignoring Lawrence because it
>   deemed him a dangerous man. This is a fine analysis of
>   Lawrence's relation with the public (as a preacher, a propagan-
>   dist, and an evangelist) and the effect of these relationships on his
>   poetry.

78. ———. "London, Midnight." *New Republic*, 16 (28
September 1918), 253.
>   Poem.

79. ———. "Once More the Georgians." Rev. of *Georgian
Poetry, 1916-1917*. *Poetry*, 12 (September 1918), 332-
37.
>   Fletcher regards the Georgians as having a proclivity for
>   bad rhymes, bad syntax, jingly meter, and subject matter
>   which is picture post-card prettiness. What Fletcher has to
>   say is particularly interesting in light of the Georgian influence
>   on his own *The Book of Nature* (1913). See I-A-1.

80. ———. "The Young Poets of Today." *Youth: Poetry of
Today*, 1 (October 1918), 12-15.
>   Essay. "The younger poets of England are less content than
>   their predecessors with easy compromises and traditional
>   forms and ideas; they are developing into ardent experimenters
>   and restless rebels." This is a cursory look at the wartime
>   English poetry scene. Poets discussed include Sacheverell
>   Sitwell, Susan Miles, Helen Hamilton, Charlotte Mew, Marion
>   Pryse, and Helen Dircks.

81. ———. "The True Conquerer," "Moods," and "The Endless Lament." *Literary Digest,* 59 (9 November 1918), 26.

Poems. Reprinted from *Japanese Prints* (1918). See I-A-8.

82. ———. "The Passing of the Armies." *Youth: Poetry of Today,* 1 (December 1918), 38-41.

Poem.

83. ———. "Peace," "The Red Gates," and "Pictures: Tendencies in Present-Day English Art." *Pictures, 1917-1918,* Ed. C. W. Beaumont and M.T.H. Sadler. London. C. W. Beaumont, 1918. pp. 26-29, 112-19.

Poems and Essay. "Peace" and "The Red Gates" are poems. In "Pictures: Tendencies in Present-Day English Art" Fletcher maintains that English art has always been a matter of individuals rather than schools. England's insular geography protects her from the weaker and more irresponsible currents of art which too readily sway the Continent. Considers Alfred Stevens, John Constable, Walter Sickert, Augustus John, C. J. Holmes, Wilson Steer, Paul Nash, Eric Gill, among others.

84. ———. "A Rational Explanation of *Vers Libre.*" *Dial,* 66 (11 January 1919), 11-13.

Essay. A defense of free verse by a practitioner. Interestingly refers to the Imagists as "they". Presents five "laws" which govern the writing of free verse.

85. ———. "Perfume of Cathay." Rev. of *Chinese Poems* tr. by Arthur Waley. *Poetry,* 13 (February 1919), 273-81.

Interesting in that Fletcher focuses on the Oriental point of view. He tries to implement this in his own work, particularly in *Japanese Prints.* See I-A-8.

86.   ———. "Cultivation and the Wild in Contemporary English Poetry." *Youth: Poetry of Today,* 1 (April 1919), 83-86.

Essay. The increase in the stream of poetry during the last twenty years is due, in part, to a reaction against industrialism, a reaction to the crazes of the early 90s, and a reaction partly to Wordsworthian insularity.

87.   ———. "The Silent Navy." *Yale Review,* 8 (April 1919), 466-67.

Poem.

88.   ———. "Old England." Rev. of *Last Poems* by Edward Thomas. *Poetry,* 14 (May 1919), 103-06.

Draws some very interesting parallels to Robert Frost. Otherwise a nondescript review, perhaps revealing Fletcher's perception of the Englishman's propensity to die for his country.

89.   ———. "Conrad Aiken—Metaphysical Poet." Rev. of *The Charnel Rose* by Conrad Aiken. *Dial,* 66 (31 May 1919), 558-59.

Essay. A critical treatment of what Fletcher sees as a metaphysical strain running through Aiken's poetry. The use of the term *metaphysical* is particularly interesting as it pre-dates by two years T.S. Eliot's revival of the term in his now famous essay.

90.   ———. "The Giants." *Youth: Poetry of Today,* 1 (June 1919), 89-90.

Poem.

91.   ———. "The Poetry of André Fontainas." *New World,* 1 (June-July 1919), 258-69.

Essay. A rather cursory overview of Fontainas's work and career. Basically this is an English version of *La Poésie d'André Fontainas.* See I-A-10.

92.   ———. "Earth." *Yale Review*, 8 (July 1919), 772-75.
       Poem.

93.   ———. "A Jazz Critic." Rev. of *The New Era in
       American Poetry*, by Louis Untermeyer. *Dial*, 67 (23
       August 1919), 155-56.
       Delineates three basic types of criticism. Highly critical of
       Untermeyer's view of American poetry; see II-B-83.

94.   ———. "At Sunrise" and "The Forest of Night."
       Coterie, No. 2, September 1919, pp. 20-22.
       Poems. "At Sunrise" is reprinted in *The Black Rock* (1928), and
       in *A Miscellany of American Poetry 1920*, p. 33. See I-A-16 and
       I-B-118.

95.   ———. "The Stone Place" and "Gates." *Coterie*, No.
       3, December 1919, pp. 7-8.
       Poems. "Gates" is reprinted in *The Black Rock* (1928). "The
       Stone Place" is reprinted in *A Miscellany of American Poetry 1920*,
       p. 36. See I-A-16 and I-B-118.

96.   ———. "The Time of the Year" and "Rain." *Poetry*,
       15 (December 1919), 142-48.
       Poems.

97.   ———. "The Spirit of the Old Hotel." *Dial*, 68
       (January 1920), 77-79.
       Prose. An experiment with mood.

98.   ———. "The Structure of Chinese Poetry." Rev. of
       More Translations from the Chinese by Arthur Waley.
       Dial, 68 (February 1920), 263-66.
       Interesting when juxtaposed against Fletcher's own interest
       in oriental poetry and its influence on his own poetry.

99.   ———. "The Drawing of Jean de Bosschère."
       International Studio, 70 (March 1920), 193-201.
       Essay. Critical assessment of de Bosschère's work. Of

particular note is Fletcher's focus on de Bosschère's theory concerning the separateness of color and appearance— applicable to artist, poet, and prosewriter.

100. ———. "From Babel's Night," "The Eagles," "London Nightfall," and "The Bridge." *Coterie*, No. 4, Easter 1920, pp. 37-39.

    Poems. "London Nightfall" is reprinted in *The Black Rock* (1928) and *Selected Poems* (1938); cf. "London Evening" and "London Night," *The Dominant City* (1913). "The Bridge" is reprinted in *The Black Rock* (1928). See I-A-16, I-A-23, and I-A-2.

101. ———. "In the City of Night." *Anglo-French Review*, 3 (April 1920), 272-74.

    Poem. Reprinted from *The Dominant City (1911-1912)* (1913); reprinted in *Breakers and Granite* (1921). See I-A-2 and I-A-11.

102. ———. "Thomas Hardy's Poetry." Rev. of *Collected Poems* by Thomas Hardy. *Poetry*, 16 (April 1920), 43-49.

    Views Hardy as the most "homogeneous" of all English poets.

103. ———. "Some Contemporary American Poets." *Chapbook*, May 1920, pp. 1-31.

    Essay. Examines the contemporary revival in American poetry, tracing its origins to Edwin Arlington Robinson's *The Children of the Night*. In the course of this very important essay Robinson, Frost, Amy Lowell, Edgar Lee Masters, Sandburg, Vachel Lindsay, Pound, Aiken, Stevens, and Kreymborg are all given attention. Reprinted as a monograph by: Folcroft, Pa.: Folcroft Library Editions, 1975; Norwood, Pa.: Norwood Editions, 1976; and Philadelphia, Pa.: R. West, 1977.

104. ———. "Gulf Stream." *Athenaeum*, No. 4701 (4 June 1920), 729.

    Poem. Reprinted in *The Black Rock* (1928) and *Selected Poems* (1938). See I-A-16 and I-A-23.

105.   ———. "Passing of the West." *New Republic*, 23 (23 June 1920), 124-26.

Essay. Almost a prose poem with its rich description based in the historical development of the American West. Done for effect, not argument.

106.   ———. "Mr. Lawrence's New Poems." Rev. of *New Poems* by D. H. Lawrence. *Freeman*, 1 (21 July 1920), 451-52.

Lawrence's work represents a narrow but valid line of progress in English poetry.

107.   ———. "Two Minor Poets." Rev. of *A Canticle of Pan* by Witter Bynner and *The Little Red School* by T. Sturge Moore. *Freeman*, 1 (28 July 1920), 476-77.

Fletcher tells us that "the great poet transmutes his sentiment into something higher and finer. He is capable of dealing with the unfused and confusing generalizations of mere sentiment, for the reason that they are too common and do not insistently demand expression."

108.   ———. "The Black Rock: To Thomas Hardy." *Yale Review*, 9 (July 1920), 727-31.

Poem. Reprinted in *Yale Review*, 17 (April 1928), pp. 447-51. See also I-B-119 and "The Black Rock" in *The Black Rock* (1928), I-A-16.

109.   ———. "The Wanderer." *New Republic*, 24 (22 September 1920), 99.

Poem. Reprinted in *The Black Rock* (1928). See I-A-16

110.   ———. "Anthologia Contra Mundum." Rev. of *Modern British Poetry: A Collection* ed. Louis Untermeyer. *Freeman*, 2 (13 October 1920), 116.

Compliments Untermeyer on his inclusions, and takes him to task on his omissions.

111. ———. "A Very Modern Leda." Rev. of *Leda* by Aldous Huxley, *Freeman*, 2 (20 October 1920), 141.

Chides Huxley for writing within a tradition instead of as he really feels.

112. ———. "Some Defects of Genius." Rev. of *Enslaved* by John Masefield. *Freeman*, 2 (27 October 1920), 163.

Observes that the only intelligent way to worship beauty is to create it. Criticism of art must examine truth, passion, and sincerity which are fundamental to beauty.

113. ———. "Down the Mississippi." *Poetry*, 17 (October 1920), 1-5.

Poem. Comprised of "Embarkation," "Heat," "Full Moon," "The Moon's Orchestra," "The Stevedores," "Night Landing," and "The Silence." This poem catches the flavor of America and marks the beginning of the poet's movement back to his American roots. Reprinted in *Breakers and Granite* (1921) and *Selected Poems* (1938). See I-B-363. Also see I-A-11, I-A-23, I-B-360.

114. ———. "John Masefield: A Study." *North American Review*, 212 (October 1920), 548-51.

Essay. Ranks Masefield with Hardy among living English poets. Traces Masefield's transition from the romantic realist towards fatalism and skepticism.

115. ———. "Verses Polite and Impolite." Rev. of *Poems: 1916-1918* by Francis Brett Young and *Argonaut and Juggernaut* by Osbert Sitwell. *Freeman*, 2 (3 November 1920), 189-90.

Fletcher tells us that "every experience is, or should be, important to a true poet." The observation that below a certain level, all poets are on a par with each other is Fletcher's final verdict.

116. ———. "The Work of J.C. Squire." Rev. of *The Birds and Other Poems* by J.C. Squire. *Freeman*, 2 (1 December 1920), 284-85.

Fletcher discusses "objectivity" and "subjectivity" in Squire's poetry and their consequent effect on the personality of his poetry.

117. ———. "Contemporary Poets." Rev. of *Aurelia and Other Poems* by Robert Nichols. *Freeman*, 2 (15 December 1920), 331.

Traces Nichols's poetic heritage to the Elizabethans and one or two French symbolists, with an undertone of violent Keatsian lyricism.

118. ———. "At Sunrise," "Noon," "The Stone Place," "The Day that Autumn Came," "The Tower," "The Swan," "Sunset," "The Star," "Exit," "The Homecoming," "Blake," "Advent," "The Road," and "Kingdoms." *A Miscellany of American Poetry 1920*. New York: Harcourt, Brace and Howe, 1920. pp. 33-49.

Poems. All poems are reprinted in *The Black Rock* (1928). In addition: "Sunrise" is reprinted from *Coterie*, September 1919; "The Stone Place" is reprinted from *Coterie*, December 1919; "The Swan," "Sunset," "Exit," and "Blake" are reprinted in *Selected Poems* (1938), see also I-C-7; "Advent" is reprinted in *Selected Poems* (1938) and in *Current Opinion*, November 1920, p. 715; see I-A-23.

119. ———. "Forward" and "The Black Rock: To Thomas Hardy." *American and British Verse from the Yale Review*. New Haven: Yale University Press, 1920. pp. [5]-6, 26-31.

Essay and poem. Fletcher presents his view that American literature ought not be considered as something entirely separate from British literature—they have a common bond in a common language.

120. ———. "The Stars" and "Who Will Mark." *Coterie*, No. 6 & 7, Winter 1920-21, pp. 32-33.

Poems. "The Stars" is reprinted in *The Black Rock* (1928). See I-A-16.

121. ———. "Mr. Drinkwater's Pawns." Rev. of *Pawns* by John Drinkwater. *Freeman*, 2 (5 January 1921), 405.

Fletcher delineates between the poetic and dramatic elements of poetic drama.

122. ———. "A Question of Attitude." Rev. of *Collected Poems* by Walter de la Mare. *Freeman*, 2 (26 January 1921), 477-78.

Fletcher postulates that "the great poets have always succeeded in making their art imply an equal acceptance of the grim business of living."

123. ———. "The Enduring." *Athenaeum*. No. 4735 (28 January 1921), 93.

Poem. Reprinted in *Living Age*, 308 (5 March 1921), p. 620; *Literary Digest*, 19 March 1921, p. 38; and *Breakers and Granite* (1921) and *Selected Poems* (1938). See I-A-11 and I-A-23. See I-B-170.

124. ———. "A French View of Poe." Rev. of *La Vie d'Edgar A. Poe* by André Fontainas. *Yale Review*, 10 (January 1921), 444-48.

Fletcher's own high regard for Poe, a fellow Southerner, is evident.

125. ———. "Old Age Echoes." Rev. of *October* by Robert Bridges; *Flowers and the Grass* by Maurice Hewlett; *The Country Town* by W. J. Courthorpe; and *Lines of Life* by H. W. Nevinson. *Freeman*, 2 (9 February 1921), 523-24.

A book by book assessment of worth which does not venture into theory.

126.   ———. "That Neighborly Feeling." Rev. of *Neighbors* by Wilfred Wilson Gibson. *Freeman*, 2 (23 February 1921), 571.

> Fletcher offers the opinion that nothing is so unfortunate for a poet as to have a highly adaptable temperament *and* a considerable facility in writing. The temptation is to write popular poetry.

127.   ———. "Mr. Masefield's Way." Rev. of *Right Royal* by John Masefield. *Freeman*, 2 (9 March 1921), 621.

> Suggests that here at least, Masefield's craft and polish deceives the reader into believing that this is good poetry.

128.   ———. "Scattered Gleams." Rev. of *Passenger* by Helen Dircks. *Freeman*, 3 (16 March 1921), 21-22.

> Fletcher attempts to delineate between the masculine and feminine natures in poets.

129.   ———. "Walt Whitman's Beginnings." Rev. of *The Gathering of Forces: Walt Whitman*, ed. John Black and Cleveland Rogers. *Freeman*, 3 (4 May 1921), 188.

> Emphasizes the religious quality of the world's great poems. Also presents a formula by which to judge great poetry.

130.   ———. [Untitled]. Rev. of *Kora In Hell: Improvisations* by William Carlos Williams. *Freeman*, 3 (18 May 1921), 238.

> Reprinted in *Contact* (1922), p. 15 with title "The Italics are Gods."

131.   ———. "Art and Life." *Freeman*, 3 (25 May 1921), 247.

> Essay. An attempt to define art as "life, life heightened to the point of imaginative realization the essential quality of experience sublimated by being consciously recreated." Fletcher's views about suicide expounded here are extremely portentious.

132.   ———. "The Apple" and "The Monument." *Voices*, 5 (Summer 1921), 79.

> Poems.

133. ———. "The Great War Poet." Rev. of *Poems* by
Wilfred Owen. *Freeman*, 3 (1 June 1921), 282-83.

A critical assessment of Owen, whom Fletcher judges to be a
great poet due to the enormity of his subject matter.

134. ———. "Skyscrapers." *Survey*, 46 (18 June 1921), 403.

Poem. Reprinted in *Breakers and Granite* (1921); see I-A-11.

135. ———. "The Artist's Conscience." *Freeman*, 3 (29
June 1921), 367-68.

Essay. Views the contemporary artist as needing "super-
human courage and constancy." The artist is a product of his
environment.

136. ———. "The Plays of Stephen Phillips." Rev. of
Collected Plays by Stephen Phillips. *Freeman*, 3 (13 July
1921), 428-29.

Fletcher's discourse on Elizabethan verse drama as an
abberation from the restraint of the classical Greek theater is
interesting.

137. ———. "Respectable Poetry." Rev. of *Jake* by Eunice
Tietjens and *Poems, New and Old* by John Freeman.
Freeman, 3 (30 July 1921), 453-54.

Fletcher asserts that conformity to the great law of Philistine
respectability—the maintenance of the *status quo* at all cost, is what
caused England to neglect Blake, drive Shelley and Byron into
exile, drive Coleridge to opium, ridicule Keats's poetry, and to
pension off Southey and Wordsworth.

138. ———. "Born Out of Due Time." Rev. of *The
Wagoner and Other Poems* by Edmund Blunden. *Freeman*,
3 (3 August 1921), 500.

Fletcher speaks out against the pervasive materialism of our
time.

139. ———. "Exercises in Divinity." Rev. of *Mayfair to
Moscow: Clare Sheridan's Diary* by Clare Sheridan; and
The Divine Adventure and *The Last Knight* by Theodore

Maynard. *Freeman*, 3 (17 August 1921), 546-47.

Fletcher perceives that it is different to be a great writer and to be involved with the theological spirit. One must be able to look on all things unsentimentally.

140. ———. "Poet and Translator." Rev. of *Medallions in Clay* by Richard Aldington. *Freeman*, 4 (28 September 1921), 68.

Compares Aldington's place in modern poetry to that of Thomas Campion's in the Elizabethan period.

141. ———. "The Cataract." *Fanfare*, 1 October 1921, p. 6.

Poem. Reprinted in *The Black Rock* (1928) and *Selected Poems* (1938). See I-A-16 and I-A-23.

142. ———. "The Poetry of Edward Thomas." Rev. of *Collected Poems* by Edward Thomas. *Freeman*, 4 (19 October 1921), 140.

The nature poet always ends by revealing that all human views of nature are colored by different degrees of human experience.

143. ———. "Feminism in Poetry." Rev. of *Contemplative Quarry and the Man with a Hammer* by Anna Wickham. *Freeman*, 4 (26 October 1921), 164-65.

Good poetry is based on intensity; its ideas being strong, vital, and original, and articulate with all possible vigor of language at the poet's disposal. Fletcher finds it difficult to write truly intense lyrical poetry since the English language has degenerated into mere rhetorical formulae.

144. ———. "An Englishman in Arabia." Rev. of *Travels in Arabia Deserta* by Charles M. Doughty. *Freeman*, 4 (23 November 1921), 259-61.

Fletcher states his own suspicion of our "so-called" civilization with its overgrown development of mechanical appurtenances.

145. ———. "An English Epicurean." Rev. of *Impressions*

and Comments: Second Series by Havelock Ellis. *Freeman*, 4
(14 December 1921), 330-31.

Fletcher's Anglophilia is evident.

146.   ———. "Mr. Edwin Arlington Robinson Abroad."
Living Age, 311 (17 December 1921), 744.

Letter to the editor. Fletcher answers a critic on behalf of
Robinson's *The Man Against the Sky*.

147.   ———. "The Captive Lion." Rev. of *The Captive Lion
and Other Poems* by William Henry Davies. *Freeman*, 4
(21 December 1921), 356-57.

Fletcher exhibits sensitivity in recognizing a disproportion
between Davies's experience and that subject about which he
writes. Fletcher registeres his dissatisfaction with this poet who
has made no experiments either in subject matter or in form,
while confining himself to variations of a single theme.

148.   ———. "A Metaphysical Poet." Rev. of *The Journey:
Odes and Sonnets* by Gerald Gould. *Freeman*, 4 (28
December 1921), 379-80.

Notes that Gould is a metaphysical poet—a rare thing these
days. Fletcher laments the lack of thought in modern poetry.

149.   ———. "The Death of England," "In the Gallery of
Skulls," "The Secret of Mars," "The New World," and
"The Way of Dust." *Broom*, 1 (January 1922), 207-10.

Prose poems. All are reprinted in *Parables* (1925). See I-A-14.

150.   ———. "Last Wishes." *Broom*, 1 (January 1922), 288.

Poem.

151.   ———. "Tradition and Transition." Rev. of *Poems:
Second Series* by J. C. Squire and *The Pier-Glass* by Robert
Graves. *Freeman*, 4 (8 February 1922), 524-25.

Accuses Squires of having sacrificed too many precious
qualities of heart for the sake of blindly following a bygone
tradition. Sees Graves as still developing.

152. ———. "The Poetry of Charlotte Mew." Rev. of *Saturday Market* by Charlotte Mew. *Freeman*, 5 (15 March 1922), 20-21.

Fletcher compares Mew to Emily Dickinson. In this most complimentary review Fletcher discusses aspects of oriental poetry which he finds present in the work of Mew and Dickinson.

153. ———. "Napoleon." *Dial*, 72 (April 1922), 393-97.

Poem. c.f. "Elegy on Napoleon" in *XXIV Elegies* (1935) and *Selected Poems* (1938). See also I-A-21 and I-A-23.

154. ———. "To a Starving Man." *Broom*, 2 (April 1922), 1.

Poem.

155. ———. "Vernal Twitterings." Rev. of *China Awakened* by M.T.Z. Tyau; *Two Poems: The Red Path and the Wounded Bird* by John Freeman; and *Music* by John Freeman. *Freeman*, 5 (3 May 1922), 187-88.

Fletcher sarcastically observes that the modern minor poet is too studious of his own reputation and equally indifferent to the appeal of any poet whose work has not been sanctioned by academic approval.

156. ———. "The Quality of Shelley." Rev. of *Three Studies in Shelley* by Archibald T. Armstrong and *Shelley and Calderon* by Salvador de Madariaga. *Freeman*, 5 (24 May 1922), 258-60.

157. ———. "The Piano-Organ." *Chapbook*, May 1922, pp. 19-20.

Poem.

158. ———. "The Fortunate Island." Rev. of *Anthology of Irish Verse* by Padraic Colum. *Freeman*, 5 (28 June 1922), 378-79.

Fletcher sees Ireland's poets as having overcome a tradition of national suffering and subjugation in order to maintain their artistic integrity.

159. ———. "Two English Poets." Rev. of *Seeds of Time* by John Drinkwater and *The Veil and Other Poems* by Walter de la Mare. *Freeman*, 5 (5 July 1922), 403-04.

Fletcher is vicious in his treatment of the safeness, saneness, and tradition of Drinkwater's book.

160. ———. ["Answer to the Three Questions Regarding the Necessity, the Function, and the Form of Poetry"]. *Chapbook*, July 1922, pp. 8-9.

Essay of sorts. Fletcher, as well as other literary notables, answer questions: 1. Do you think that poetry is a necessity to modern man? 2. What in modern life is the particular function of poetry as distinguished from other kinds of literature? 3. Do you think there is any chance of verse being eventually displaced by prose, as narrative poetry apparently is by the novel, and ballads already have been by newspaper reports?

161. ———. "Dublin, July 1922." *Nation and Athenaeum*, 31 (22 July 1922), 565.

Poem. Reprinted in *Living Age*, 314 (26 August 1922), p. 552 and *Literary Digest*, 19 August 1922, p. 38.

162. ———. "San Antonio" and "Dixie." *Double Dealer*, 4 (August 1922), 63, 89.

Poems. A 1915 visit to San Antonio, Texas had indelibly impressed in the poet's mind an image of Mexican life in the Southwest. "Dixie" represents the seminal stages of a developing Southern regionalism.

163. ———. "A Poet of Fancy." Rev. of *Down-adown-Derry* by Walter de la Mare. *Freeman*, 5 (9 August 1922), 525-26.

Discusses the problems of fancy versus imagination. The poet of fancy seeks to escape reality whereas the poet of imagination strives to transform reality.

164.   ———. "Negro Folk Poetry." Rev. of *Negro Folk-Rhymes* by Thomas W. Talley. *Nation and Athenaeum*, 31 (9 September 1922), 763-64.

In a most revealing passage Fletcher theorizes that "the Negro is by nature a creature of highly developed instinct, but of small initiative. He is plastic, adaptable, quick to take a hint, imitative of any race that is his superior in energy, and capable of adjusting himself to the most unfavorable circumstances." It is this trait, Fletcher tells us, that has enabled him to endure the experience of slavery in America.

165.   ———. "Mr. Hardy's Goodbye." Rev. of *Late Lyrics and Earlier* by Thomas Hardy. *Freeman*, 6 (18 October 1922), 139.

Thinks it very sad that a man like Hardy would reproach himself because there are fools in the world who would not listen to him. This sensitiveness of nature is the manifestation of an ingrained puritanical sensitivity.

166.   ———. "A Georgian Intellectualist." Rev. of *Real Property* by Harold Monro. *Poetry*, 21 (October 1922), 38-43.

". . . the modern poet whose interests are intellectual rather than emotional, has either to invent an elaborate technique of his own, or give up writing."

167.   ———. "Incunabula." Rev. of *On English Poetry* by Robert Graves. *Freeman*, 6 (1 November 1922), 187-88.

Fletcher's view is that poets should write poetry and not write about how they write or wrote it.

168.   ———. "Irradiations" and "Epilogue." *Current Opinion*, 73 (November 1922), 654-55.

Poems. Reprinted from *Irradiations, Sand and Spray* (1915). See I-A-6.

169.   ———. "Middle Age." *Milwaukee Arts Monthly*, 1 (November-December 1922), 11-12.

Poem.

170. ———. "A Rebel," "The Rock," "Blue Water," "Prayers for the Wind," "Impromptu," "Chinese Poet Among Barbarians," "Snowy Mountains," "The Future," "Upon the Hill," and "The Enduring." *American Poetry 1922: A Miscellany.* New York: Harcourt Brace & Co., 1922. pp. 127-37.

> Poems. "A Rebel" is reprinted in *The Black Rock* (1928); "The Rock" is reprinted in *The Black Rock* (1928) and *Selected Poems* (1938); "Snowy Mountains" is reprinted in *The Black Rock* (1928); "Impromptu" is reprinted in *The Black Rock* (1928); "The Enduring" is reprinted in *The .Black Rock* (1928) and *Selected Poems* (1938). See I-A-16 and I-A-23.

171. ———. "Pauper Death." *Rhythmus,* 1 (January 1923), 546-48.

> Poem.

172. ———. "Ezra Pound." Rev. of *Poems 1918-1922* by Ezra Pound. *Prairie,* (January-February 1923), 38-39.

> Calls Pound one of the most serious writers living while pointing out that they have almost no views in common. Comments that Pound and Eliot offer modern notes of disillusionment, Pound shrinking and refining this disillusionment to a sculptural elegance.

173. ———. "Bali." Rev. of *Bali* by Gregor Krause and Karl Witz. *Freeman,* 6 (14 February 1923), 546-48.

> Fletcher holds that the old nineteenth-century chaos cannot endure. Humanity "today" is faced with a difficult alternative: either society must become dehumanized, scientific, a marvel of mechanical efficiency, or there must be a destructive reordering of society from top to bottom so that new and natural growth can take place.

174. ———. "The Last Frontier" and "Cro-Magnon." *The Fugitive,* 2 (February-March 1923), 10, 16-17.

> Poems. "The Last Frontier" is reprinted in *The Black Rock* (1928) and *Selected Poems* (1938). See I-A-16 and I-A-23.

175. ———. "A Knight-Errant of the Spirit." Rev. of
The Tragic Sense of Life by Miguel de Unamuno, tr.
Crawford Flitch. *Freeman*, 7 (28 March 1923), 65-67.

Fletcher refers to himself as a disillusioned idealist.

176. ———. "An Ultra/Modern Poet." Rev. of *Job de
Pauvre* by Jean de Bosschère. *Freeman*, 7 (11 April
1923), 116-17.

Sees contemporary poets as being either realists or
metaphysical.

177. ———. "On the Stones of the Road." Rev. of
History of Art by Élie Faure, tr. Walter Pach. *Freeman*,
7 (25 April 1923), 161-63.

Regards art as the record of what man has sought, needed,
and dreamed of through the centuries. Man's creations are his
attempt to arrest the universal flux of things, stamping on
them the image which the artist's application holds at some
particular moment. Fletcher sees Faure's book as a message to
America, that if we are to assume spiritual leadership of the
world, we must learn that every man is an artist in his own
right. This is the philosophic foundation Fletcher believes is
necessary for promoting folk art and regionalism.

178. ———. "Prayers I-XI." *Poetry*, 22 (April 1923), 6-10.

Poem(s). c.f. "Prayers to the Unknown God" in Book 5 of *The
Black Rock* (1928). See I-A-16.

179. ———. "Some Day." *Chapbook*, April 1923, p. 10.

Poem.

180. ———. "Majors and Minors." Rev. of *The Lions: A
Jungle Poem* by Edwin Curran; *Roast Leviathan* by Louis
Untermeyer; *Banners in the Dawn* and *Ebony Flame* by
Vincent Starrett; *Lute and Furrow* by Olive Tilford
Dargan; *Faces and Open Doors* by Agnes Lee; and *Songs
of Unrest* by Bernice Lesbia Kenyon. *Freeman*, 7 (9
May 1923), 212-13.

Fletcher theorizes that "even to the dullest clods and the

merest bumpkins among us, there must come moments when
the passion and energy that seem to be behind words in
rhythmical sequence leap out and challenge the uneasy
compromises that we call living; there are very few
beings . . . who are not potentially poets."

181.   ———. "Function of Creation." *Literary Review of the
New York Evening Post*, 3 (26 May 1923), 713-14.
   Essay. Fletcher lashes out at the desire of critics to dissect
the artist in order to discover the essence of his art. He
attempts to dispel some common misperception that the public
has about artists. The classification of the moral usefulness of
art is presented under three headings: 1. "art as moral
prophylaxis; 2. art as catharsis; and 3. the unmoral usefulness
of art may be generally summed up under the heading of art as
stimulant."

182.   ———. "Vincent Van Gogh." Rev. of *Vincent Van
Gogh: A Biographical Study* by Julius Meier-Graefe, tr.
John Holroyd Reece. *Freeman*, 7 (30 May 1923), 281-
83.
   Fletcher presents a straight biographical synopsis of Van
Gogh's life.

183.   ———. "Three Women Poets." Rev. of *Black
Armour* by Elinor Wylie; *April Twilights* by Willa
Cather; and *Sea Change* by Muna Lee. *Freeman*, 7 (18
July 1923), 452.
   Fletcher finds that the "profound sexual differences which
exist between the nature of woman and that of man" manifest
themselves in the attitude towards life which is displayed by
the two sexes.

184.   ———. "The Autumn Horsemen." *Measure*, July
1923, pp. 12-13.
   Poem.

185.   ———. "Mirthful Verses." Rev. of *Imperial
Fiddlesticks* by Herbert W. Hartman; *Going-to-the-Sun*
by Vachel Lindsay; *Galimathias* by Matthew

Josephson, and *The Ballad of William Sycamore* by
Stephen Vincent Benét. *Freeman*, 7 (1 August 1923),
499-500.

Light treatment of what Fletcher regards as light verse.
However, his introductory comments on the "art" of humor
are most interesting.

186.   ———. "Out Where the West Begins." Rev. of
Selected Poems by George Sterling and *The Poetical
Works of Joaquin Miller* by Joaquin Miller. *Freeman*, 7
(15 August 1923), 548-49.

More important than Fletcher's lack of appreciation for the
poems of Miller and Sterling is his view that in spite of the
material success of the pioneers of 1849 their spiritual failure
was as complete as history ever recorded. "The pioneers did
not understand that which opposed their migration was not
the Indians, but rather "the Wind-Spirit, the Rain-God, and the
Thunder-Bird in person."

187.   ———. "Ibsen's Living Plays." Rev. of *Peer Gynt* by
Henrik Ibsen. *Freeman*, 7 (29 August 1923), 595-96.

"All great art," Fletcher tells us, "depends upon having ideas;
ideas that despite the fact that their creator has passed away,
still emerge from the past to speak to us. The creation of a
masterpiece of literature is to the author the accomplishment
of a successful love-affair: it is a thing on which he feels he can
spend an infinite degree of pains, and which only the limitations
of his physical strength forbid him to think of a being ever
complete."

188.   ———. "American Regionalism." Rev. of *Maine
Coast* by Wilbert Snow; *Carolina Chansons* by DuBose
Heyward and Hervey Allen; and *The American
Rhythm* by Mary Austin. *Freeman*, 7 (5 September
1923), 621-22.

"One of the most interesting and pathetic features of
American literature is its insistence, not upon what is universal
and peculiar to the United States as a whole, but only what is
accidental and transitory, some freak of local color."

189. ———. "St. Paul's Chapel, New York." *Literary Review of the New York Evening Post*, 4 (5 September 1923), 17.

Poem.

190. ———. "Safe and Sane Romanticism." Rev. of *Collected Poems* by Vachel Lindsay. *Freeman*, 8 (12 September 1923), 22-23.

Fletcher focuses on Lindsay's religion. He is viewed as a Protestant that is practically empty of every intellectual or moral issue in life peculiarly American. Fletcher says, "beyond politics, temperance, the ecstasy of avowing oneself a saved soul, and the feeling of individual exposiveness that is so proudly called 'one-hundred-per-cent Americanism'." There is a sureness that the world will experience salvation which is reflected in Lindsay's poetry. He compares Lindsay with E. A. Robinson with some interesting insights.

191. ———. "The Impasse of Civilization." Rev. of *The Dance of Life* by Havelock Ellis. *Freeman*, 8 (24 October 1923), 162-64.

Fletcher draws a comparison between "now" and the days shortly before the breakup of the Roman Empire. Man has become generally more eager to spend his time thinking about existence, about good and evil, God and soul, than to enjoy this existence untrammelled by such speculations. Fletcher's extreme dissatisfaction with the world in which he lives is very evident.

192. ———. "William Blake." *North American Review*, 218 (October 1923), 518-28.

Essay. Fletcher was impressed by Blake's concept of working "an allegory addressed to the intellectual understanding."

193. ———. "The Revival of Aestheticism." Rev. of *Harmonium* by Wallace Stevens; *The Pilgrimage of Festus* by Conrad Aiken; *Less Lonely* by Alfred Kreymborg; *Charlatan* by Louis Grudin; *Cups of Illusion* by Henry

Bellaman; and *In Exile* by John Cournos. *Freeman*, 8
(19 December 1923), 355-56.

Fletcher writes that it is a paradox of life that beauty, like
happiness, if directly aimed at us, eludes us. Therefore the
artist who makes beauty unsupported by thought his sole aim
inevitably writes incidental trifles. Fletcher is astute in his
recognition of Steven's talent in *Harmonium*, his first book.
Although judging him to be a aesthete—he is an honest
aesthete.

194.   ———. "The Wreck." *Bookman*, 58 (December
1923), 417.

Poem.

195.   ———. "The Will and the Brain." *Freeman*, 8 (9
January 1924), 427.

Letter to editor. Fletcher replies to William C. Kinstad's
letter in 28 November issue of *Freeman* in which he had called to
question Fletcher's review of Havelock Ellis's *The Dance of Life*
based on the distinction between the will and brain. Fletcher
goes on record as favoring a race of supermen which can be
accomplished only if we can liberate the will from the brain in
the ordinary affairs of life, as it is liberated already at moments
of great stress and strain.

196.   ———. "The Downfall of Civilization: Mechanical
Industrialization and the Progressive Enslavement
of Men's Souls." *New York Times*, 13 January 1924,
Section 6, p. 6.

Essay. A pessimistic picture of what Fletcher views as a
current trend. This article is in response to a request by the
Times that he fully explain a recent and much discussed
statement to the effect that this is a non civilized age.

197.   ———. "Sentiment and Anti-Sentiment." Rev. of
Tulips and Chimneys by E. E. Cummings and *The Harp-*

Weaver and Other Poems by Edna St. Vincent Millay.
Freeman, 8 (30 January 1924), 502.

Some interesting perceptions on the fine line between
sentiment and sentimentality.

198.　────. "The Lovers." *Lyric*, 4 (January 1924), 2.

Poem. Reprinted in *Literary Digest*, 21 January 1924, p. 34.

199.　────. "The Spirit of Thomas Hardy." *Yale Review*,
13 (January 1924), [322]-33.

Essay. Critical evaluation of Hardy and his poetry. Places
Hardy in the pantheon of his nineteenth and twentieth-
century contemporaries.

200.　────. "The Question of Environment." Rev. of
New Hampshire by Robert Frost. *Freeman*, 8 (27
February 1924), 593-94.

The American poet, in Fletcher's view, is in the tragic
position of having to create, not only his poems, but also the
environment from which the work springs. America is seen as
an environment which reacts negatively to art and is at best
capable of producing only a negative masterpiece—*Spoon River*,
for instance. America, for all its recent cultural advances, is still
the land of culturally starved lives. Frost's fortunes in
accidentally discovering a comfortable environment have ended
with his having to endure an environment which dictates to
him that which he should write.

201.　────. "Minor Poetry." Rev. of *Body of This Death* by
Louise Bogan; *Masquerade* by Ben Ray Redman;
Lackeys of the Moon by Mary Cass Canfield; *The Ancient
Beautiful Things* by Fannie Stearns Davis; and *Gipsy
Gold* by Charles Divine. *Freeman*, 8 (5 March 1924),
622.

Fletcher examines the role of the minor poet in the present
age of spiritual sterility and outward industry.

202. ———. "Walt Whitman." *North American Review*, 219 (March 1924), 355-66.

Essay. Whitman is viewed as the "only democratic poet the world has ever possessed." Fletcher takes to task those critics who have not given Whitman the credit deserved.

203. ———. "The Spirit of Seven Poets." Rev. of *The Pilgrimage of Festus* by Conrad Aiken; *The Ballad of Saint Barbara* by G. K. Chesterton; *The Dream and Other Poems* by John Masefield; *Real Property* by Harold Monro; *Roast Leviathan* by Louis Untermeyer; *At the Roots of the Grass* by Muriel Strode; and *Black Armour* by Elinor Wylie. *Yale Review*, 13 (April 1924), 585-88.

Defines the final absolute illusion of art, whereby we see certain things done, and do not know how they are done, but can only murmur how beautiful they are.

204. ———. "The Woodcuts of John J. A. Murphy." *Print Collector's Quarterly*, 11 (April 1924), 227-52.

Essay. Fletcher's insights on the effectiveness of contrasting black and white is important to his own early work. The first paragraph contains exquisitely poetic prose. Fletcher's sensitivity for Murphy's creation of visual rhythms indicates his own success in synthesis of rhythmic patterns for effect.

205. ———. "American Poetry." *Literary Review of the New York Evening Post*, 4 (21 June 1924), 833-34.

Essay. Argues that there is an American tradition in poetry—particularly a distinctive American rhythm.

206. ———. "Blake the Philosopher." Rev. of *William Blake: His Philosophy and Symbols* by S. Foster Damon. *New Republic*, 39 (20 August 1924), 366-67.

Fletcher states that of the nineteenth century, only Leopardi, Schopenhauer, James Thomson, Melville, Whitman, Shelley, and Blake give us an honest, and not morally crooked, vision of life.

207. ———. "Woman and Poet." Rev. of *Life and Letters of Emily Dickinson* by Martha Dickinson Bianchi and *The Complete Poems of Emily Dickinson*. *Saturday Review of Literature*, 1 (30 August 1924), 77-78.

One must wonder to what degree there is empathy in Fletcher's evaluation that Emily Dickinson was born "as so many geniuses are, of parents who utterly failed to comprehend her, but whose chief merit is that they did not oppose her. . . ." In addition, Fletcher presents some interesting alternatives regarding God-man relationships.

208. ———. "From Portofino Point (In Memoriam, Friedrich Nietzsche). *Buccaneer*, 1 (November 1924), 2-5.

Poem. Reprinted in *The Black Rock* (1928) and *Selected Poems* (1938). See I-A-16 and I-A-23.

209. ———. "Midwinter." *Saturday Review of Literature*, 1 (3 January 1925), 425.

Poem.

210. ———. "The Oarsman." *Guardian*, 1 (March 1925), 185-86.

Poem.

211. ———. "The Seven Cities of Cibola." *Southwest Review*, 10 (April 1925), 3-7.

Poem. Includes "Prelude," I. "Babel, The Great City," II. "The Beautiful City," III. "Deseret, The Sorrowful City," IV. "The Haunted City," V. "Granath, The Inaccessible City," VI. "The Populous City," and VII. "The Sublime City."

212. ———. "May Night." *Philadelphia Public Ledger Literary Review*, 3 May 1925, p. 5.

Poem.

213. ———. "Jason at Corinth." *Guardian*, 2 (May-June 1925), 185-86.

Poem.

214. ———. Rev. of *History of Art* by Élie Faure, tr. by
Walter Pach. *Yale Review*, 14 (July 1925), 805-09.

Fletcher reveals his opinion on the dilemma of the
contemporary artist.

215. ———. "Amy Lowell: A Reminiscence." *Guardian*, 2
(August 1925), 345-48.

Essay. Amy Lowell had a profound influence on Fletcher's
early career and his association with the Imagist movement.
This is, in effect, an eulogy upon her recent death.

216. ———. "The American Mind: The Background." *The
New Age*, 38 (17 December 1925), 76-77.

Essay. Fletcher winces at the American tendency to exalt the
"red-neck," "the hick," "the go-getter," and the "grafter."
Fletcher sees America as insensitive to its own cultural
antecedents, hellbent to adopt European affectation, and to
embrace technology in lieu of its agrarian origins. He presents
here an America from which he had expatriated himself. See I-
B-217, 218, 219, 220, and 221 for other parts of this essay.

217. ———. "The American Mind: Dollar Democracy."
The New Age, 38 (24 December 1925), 89-90.

Essay. Fletcher states that "socially" the American does not
exist. Vital and original types such as Whitman, Lincoln,
Melville, and Grant, begat no successors. Instead they were
replaced by hordes of immigrant strikebreakers who allowed
themselves to be used by the financier and industrialist. He
goes on to examine, what in his view were the real reasons for
American involvement in the First World War—i.e., economic
interests. His cynical assessment is that American values have
been reduced to dollar values. Everyone must work for a living,
therefore the poor man is perceived as a loafer. See I-B-216,
218, 219, 220, and 221 for other parts of this essay.

218. ———. "The American Mind: Religion and Education." *The New Age*, 38 (31 December 1925), 100-101.

Essay. Points out the hypocrisy of the desire of Americans
for religion and education, neither of which have much hold on

them. Other Fletcherisms included are: "The American
Socialist is a socialist because he hates wealth, not because he
admires the working-classes. The American atheist denies God
because he obscurely realises [sic] that the god which his people
worship is the mammon of cheap and common success.
Transport the American socialist to Europe and he becomes the
ultimate aristocrat. Transport the American atheist to Europe
and he becomes a mystic of the Middle Ages." Perhaps,
Fletcher muses, that Walt Whitman was the nearest thing to a
religious leader America has had. See I-B-216, 217, 219, 220
and 221 for other parts of this essay.

219. ———. "The American Mind: Husbands and Wives."
The New Age, 38 (7 January 1926), 112-13.

   Essay. The American woman is the means by which culture
enters the home—via social clubs. Hence she is put on a
pedestal by her sons who perpetrate this exaltation with their
own wives. Fletcher's pronouncements on the mother-child
relationship is interesting in light of the fact that some critics
have attributed an Oedipal complex to Fletcher himself. See I-
B-216, 217, 218, 220, and 221 for other parts of this essay.

220. ———. "The American Mind: Lawlessness." *The New
Age*, 38 (14 January 1926), 124-25.

   Essay. Fletcher views the American proclivity for lawlessness
as a "safety-valve for the American mind," releasing it from the
daily monotony of life's struggle. Views the disparity between
America's vitality and potential and its spiritual and cultural
barrenness as producing powerful frustration. See I-B-216, 217,
218, 219, and 221 for other parts of this essay.

221. ———. "The American Mind: Nihilism." *The New
Age*, 38 (21 January 1926), 137.

   Essay. This segment concludes the six part essay on the
American mind. Fletcher evokes Van Wyck Brooks in drawing
a parallel between the present intellectual "mental state" of
America and that of Russia at the outbreak of the revolution.
America wishes to intellectualize the past, present and future.
See I-B-216, 217, 218, 219, and 220 for other parts of this
essay.

222. ——. "The River Flows." *Criterion*, 4 (January 1926), 46-47.

> Poem. Part of a longer poem. "Autobiography," which appears in *American Caravan* (1927), *The Black Rock* (1928), and *Selected Poems* (1938). See I-A-16, I-A-23, I-B-249.

223. ——. "The Star-Scatterer." *Bucaneer*, 2 (January-March 1926), 4-5.

> Poem. c.f. "Prelude: The Star-Scatterer" in *The Black Rock* (1928), I-A-16.

224. ——. "That Day." *New Coterie*, No. 2, Spring 1926, pp. 31-32.

> Poem. Reprinted in *The Black Rock* (1928) and *Selected Poems* (1938). See I-A-16 and I-A-23.

225. ——. "America and the Future." *The New Age*, 39 (3 June 1926), 46.

> Essay. Fletcher distills from the contemporary human condition the question, "can we believe sufficiently in ourselves, in human flesh and blood and consciousness, to recreate faith? And if we can, can we induce America or Russia to believe it." This essay is quite disjointed when Fletcher engages in economic theory. See I-B-226, 227, 228, and 229 for other parts of this essay.

226. ——. "Germany and the Future of Europe: I." *The New Age*, 39 (5 August 1926), 153-54.

> Essay. Fletcher finds no one European spirit—but rather only Europeans living in various countries, each revelling in a particular national heritage. Fletcher traces the infusion of Christianity into Europe through the breakup of the Roman Empire, concluding that it was nothing but the German spirit, Teutondom, which carried the new wine into the world, and which maintained it for the nineteen centuries since. See I-B-225, 227, 228, and 229 for other parts of this essay.

227. ——. "Germany and the Future of Europe: II." *The New Age*, 39 (12 August 1926), 163-64.

Essay. Fletcher traces the influence of the German peoples on all cultural aspects of medieval Europe. Out of the struggle of the Reformation Fletcher sees Germany's "unequalled" development as an art producing nation. He perceives that the future of a less fragmented Europe lies now, as it did after the Napoleonic Wars, with Germany. See I-B-225, 226, 228, and 229 for other parts of this essay.

228. ——. "Germany and the Future of Europe: III." *The New Age*, 39 (19 August 1926), 178.

Essay. Takes issue with the Belloc-Chesterton school of historians by speaking well of the Hohenzollern monarchy. Fletcher connects the flowering of the arts with the sense of self-possession that the reign of Frederick the Great gave to the nation. He goes on to assert that the spiritual values of Germany have to be spread over the Continent before Europe can become whole and healed in order to resist the oncoming onslaughts of Russia and America. See I-B-225, 226, 227, and 229 for other parts of this essay.

229. ——. "Germany and the Future of Europe: IV." *The New Age*, 39 (26 August 1926), 190.

Essay. "Every great European soul that England has produced in the nineteenth century has been made to suffer by English provinciality and Philistinism. But every one that Germany has produced has been European first, and German afterwards—from the nineteenth century to the present day the European genius has been the German genius." States his belief in the importance of Keyserling and Spengler. See I-B-225, 226, 227, and 228 for other parts of this essay.

230. ——. "The Decline of the West." Rev. of *The Decline of the West* by Oswald Spengler. *The New Age*, 39 (2 September 1926), 203-04.

Fletcher focuses on Spengler's concern for the past, not the material past, but rather the "over-soul" of the human condition viewed in retrospect. Fletcher supports Spengler's book in the face of the three prime arguments made against it.

231.   ———. "Farewell to Europe."*The New Age*, 39 (7 October 1926), 264.

Essay. Represents an apology for his declining to review *Plato's American Republic* by Douglas Woodruff before returning to America. In a burst of chauvinism Fletcher defends America against European hypocrisy.

232.   ———. "Letter to the Editor." *Criterion*, 4 (October 1926), 746-50.

Concerning Henri Massis' *Defense of the West*.

233.   ———. "Tara is Grass." Rev. of *The Collected Poems of James Stephens* by James Stephens. *Saturday Review of Literature*, 3 (27 November 1926), 334.

Sees the writers of the Irish literary movement as being afraid of the "coarseness, hardness, and vulgarity" of life and therefore removed from it. The trouble with this age is not its speed, but its superficiality, hence we have become too passive.

234.   ———. "December." *Nature*, 8 (December 1926), 327.

Poem.

235.   ———. "To the Unknown God, I-IV." *Poetry*, 29 (December 1926), 119-28.

Poems. c.f. Book 5: "Prayers to the Unknown God," *The Black Rock* (1928), I-A-16.

236.   ———. "From 75 B.C. to 1925 A.D." Rev. of *Palimpsest* by H.D. *Saturday Review of Literature*, 3 (1 January 1927), 482.

H.D.'s first novel. Fletcher prefers H.D. the poet to the prose writer. Judges this book on the basis of her genius for lyric poetry rather than skill as prose writer.

237.   ———. "Perennial Hardy." Rev. of *The Collected Poems of Thomas Hardy* by Thomas Hardy. *Saturday*

Review of Literature, 3 (12 February 1927), 576.

Views Hardy as an impressionist in vision and an individualist in philosophy. Hardy is very much respected by Fletcher.

238. ————. "Ballad of the First Emperor." *Transition,* No. 2 (May 1927), 119-24.

Poem.

239. ————. "The Unfamiliar House." *Nation,* 125 (10 August 1927), 130.

Poem. Reprinted in *Literary Digest* (3 September 1927), p. 37; and in *South Star* (1941). See I-A-24.

240. ————. "Song of Progress." *G. K.'s Weekly,* 5 (27 August 1927), 574.

Poem. Reprinted in *Literary Digest,* 15 October 1927, p. 36, and in *The Black Rock* (1928). See also I-A-16.

241. ————. "Two Elements of Poetry." *Saturday Review of Literature,* 4 (27 August 1927), 65-66.

Essay. Raises the question of how to construct poetry out of purely intellectual subject matter, and how much depends on the feeling of the poet. Concludes that the modern poet, in order to conform to the age, must be intellectual first and emotional second.

242. ————. "Transatlantic." *Criterion,* 6 (August 1927), 128-30.

Poem.

243. ————. Rev. of *Poems* by Robert Graves; *The Clyde-Feast and Other Poems* by Sacheverell Sitwell; *Two Gentlemen in Bonds* by John Crowe Ransom; *The Close Chaplet* by Laura Riding Gottschalk; *The City* by Ruth Manning Sanders; and *Babel* by J. Redwood Anderson. *Criterion,* 6 (August 1927), 168-72.

Fletcher's own biases inevitably surface on matters of what poetry is and should be.

244.   ———— . Rev. of *The World in the Making* by Herman
        Keyserling; *Civilization or Civilizations* by E. H.
        Goddard and P. H. Gibbons; and *Communism* by H. J.
        Laski. *Criterion,* 6 (September 1927), 261-67.

    Fletcher sees man as being naive. Deems it unfortunate that
    a Marxist proletarian revolution has taken place in Russia.
    Echoes of Spengler are pervasive in this review. Reprinted in
    Living Age, 333 (15 October 1927), pp. 723-27 under the title
    "Spengler, Marx, and Keyserling."

245.   ———— . "Leon Underwood." *The Arts,* 12 (October
        1927), 210-15.

    Essay. Basically a critical and biographical overview of
    Underwood's career. Fletcher's introduction which sets his
    perception of the milieu in which Underwood worked is
    interesting in its anthropological viewpoint. Fletcher finds the
    art of the period a manifestation of national, or "racial"
    character. In his analysis of Underwood's work Fletcher dwells
    on "flow of rhythmic lines" and "interplay of forms."

246.   ———— . "Letter to the Editor." *Criterion,* 6 (October
        1927), 546-47.

    Takes issue with Robert Graves's criticism of his review of
    Laura Riding Gottschalk's *The Close Chaplet,* in *Criterion* (August
    1927). See I-B-243.

247.   ———— . "Second Advent." *Nation,* 125 (7 December
        1927), 646.

    Poem. Reprinted in *All's Well,* 7 February 1928, p. [12?]; also
    reprinted in *The Black Rock* (1928). See I-A-16. See also I-D-2.

248.   ———— . "Introduction." *The Reveries of a Solitary* by
        Jean Jacques Rousseau. tr. John Gould Fletcher.
        New York: Brentano's, 1927.

    Fletcher favors the doctrine of the superior man as the
    answer to modern social problems—i.e., the superior man in
    the Confucian sense. See I-C-5 and I-C-6.

249. ————. "Autobiography." *The American Caravan*. ed. Van Wyck Brooks et al. New York: Macaulay, 1927. pp. 421-28.

> Poem. Comprised of "Before and After," "The River Flows," "The Ship Goes Down," and "That Which Was Left." Reprinted in *The Black Rock* (1928) and *Selected Poems* (1938). See I-A-16 and I-A-23.

250. ————. "A Tennessee Epic." Rev. of *The Tall Men: Portrait of a Tennessean* by Donald Davidson. *Nation*, 126 (18 January 1928), 71.

> Complementary of Davidson's style and his subject. Fletcher's disdain for his modern age is apparent.

251. ————. "Letter to the Editor." *Criterion*, 7 (January 1928), 62-64.

> Critical response to a letter by A. L. Rowse (see *Criterion*, December 1927, 542-45) criticizing Fletcher's review of H. J. Laski's *Communism; Criterion* (September 1927), p. 261. See I-B-244.

252. ————. "Eric Gill." *Arts Magazine*, 13 (February 1928), 92-96.

> Essay. Views Gill's sculpture against the background of Pre-Raphaelitism, especially that movement's frustrated efforts to create modern medieval art.

253. ————. "The Key to Modernist Painting." Rev. of *Cezanne: A Study of His Development* by Roger Fry and *Cezanne* by Julius Meier-Graefe. *Bookman*, 67 (April 1928), 189-91.

> Fletcher regards Cezanne as the key to modernist painting. There is a poignant remark that the art of every great artist is the exact counterpart of his career.

254. ————. "East and West." *Criterion*, 7 (June 1928), 306-24.

> Essay. Oriental thought is contrasted with Western thought; based on Henri Massis' *Defense of the West*.

255.   ———. "Song of the Moderns." *Nation,* 127 (4 July 1928), 16.

   Poem. Reprinted in *The Black Rock* (1928) and *Selected Poems* (1938). See I-A-16 and I-A-23.

256.   ———. "Magnolia." *Virginia Quarterly Review,* 4 (July 1928), 384-85.

   Poem. Reprinted in *South Star* (1941). See I-A-24.

257.   ———. "The Portrait." *Nation,* 127 (29 August 1928), [204].

   Poem.

258.   ———. Rev. of *Poetic Diction* by Owen Barfield; *The Tower* by W. B. Yeats; *The Earth for Sale* by Harold Monro; *Time Importuned* by Sylvia Townshend Warner; *The Pilgrim Shadow* by James Braddock; *To One in Heaven* by Wilbur Underwood; *Poems* by Peter Quennell; and *Notes for Poems* by William Plomer; and *Triforium* by Sherard Vines. *Criterion,* 8 (September 1928), 128-34.

   Sees contemporary poetry as nearer to a tempered logically disciplined romanticism than the classicism expounded by T. S. Eliot immediately following WW I.

259.   ———. "Paul Nash." *Arts Magazine,* 14 (October 1928), 195-99.

   Essay. Sees Nash as an artist whose interest in form and sensitivity to color was so intense that he transmitted his horror of war into patterns of somber and almost Oriental richness. Turns a poet's attention to Nash's familiarity with the "grammar of form," as well as the impersonal exploration of the range of eye sensation. Fletcher also notes the fusing of structure and word into an "emotional temperature."

260.   ———. "The House of Singing Birds." *The New American Caravan.* ed. Van Wyck Brooks et al. New York: Macaulay, 1928. pp. 512-13.

   Poem.

261.   ———. "The Christmas Tree" and "In Mount
Holly." *Virginia Quarterly Review*, 5 (January 1929),
[84]-87.

>   Poems. Both are reprinted in *South Star* (1941). See I-A-24.

262.   ———. "Thomas Hardy." *Bookman*, 68 (February
1929), 621.

>   Poem.

263.   ———. "Fierce Latinity." Rev. of *Mr. Pope & Other
Poems* by Alan Tate. *Nation*, 128 (3 April 1929), 404-
05.

>   Considers Tate as a part of the insurgent South with
>   Davidson and Ransom. Picks out "Ode to the Confederate
>   Dead" for particular praise as well as Tate's intensity of world
>   view.

264.   ———. "Gertrude Hermes and Blair Hughes-
Stanton." *Print Collector's Quarterly*, 16 (April 1929),
182-98.

>   Essay. Again Fletcher demonstrates his longtime interest in
>   the art of woodcutting. His comments on the artist's approach
>   to "lighting problems" for ultimate effect has its counterparts
>   in his own work.

265.   ———. Rev. of *Ezra Pound: Selected Poems* ed. T. S.
Eliot; *A Draft of XVI Cantos of Ezra Pound* by Ezra
Pound; and *A Draft of the Cantos XVII to XXVII* by Ezra
Pound. *Criterion*, 8 (April 1929), 514-24.

>   Labels Pound a traditionalist while examining earlier
>   influences on Pound's poetry.

266.   ———. "At the Time of the Signing of the
Kellogg Pact." *New York Herald Tribune Books*, 9 June
1929, p. 4.

>   Poem.

267.   ———. "Night-Haunted Lover." Rev. of *Collected Poems* by D. H. Lawrence. *New York Herald Tribune Books*, 14 July 1929, p. 1, 6.

Sees Lawrence's poems as manifestoes, sermons, preachments on the subject of the true aim of life—to be gained through the purging flame of sex. Lawrence consequently, is viewed as a diminished artist.

268.   ———. "A Man and a Faith Without Charity." Rev. of *John Knox: Portrait of a Calvinist* by Edwin Muir. *New York Herald Tribune: The Lively Arts and Book Review*, 25 August 1929, pp. 1, 6.

A straightforward historical synopsis of Muir's book.

269.   ———. "Two Poems." *Bookman*, 70 (September 1929), 15-[16].

Poems. 1. "To a Sea-Gull" and 2. "Under Antares."

270.   ———. Rev. of *Practical Criticism: A Study of Literary Judgment* by I. A. Richards. *Criterion*, 9 (October 1929), 162-64.

Fletcher's disdain for the general poetry reading public surfaces.

271.   ———. "Ballad of the Great Emperor." *The American Caravan*. ed. Van Wyck Brooks et al. New York: Macaulay, 1929. pp. 349-51.

Poem.

272.   ———. Rev. of *Scolastique par Jacques Maritain* by Jacques Maritain and *The Philosophy of Art: Being 'Art et Scholastique'* [sic] by Jacques Maritain, tr. Rev. John O'Connor, S. T. P. *Criterion*, 9 (January 1930), 346-49.

Outlines Maritain's thesis point by point while suggesting attention to logical difficulties he sees in Maritain's philosophy.

273. ——. "Woodcuts of Cecil Buller." *Print Collector's Quarterly,* 17 (January 1930), 92-105.

Essay. Fletcher's breadth of knowledge of this medium is obvious. Observations on relationships between form and medium are of particular interest when transferred to Fletcher's poetry.

274. ——. Rev. of *The Testament of Beauty* by Robert Bridges and *Deucalion or The Future of Literary Criticism* by Geoffrey West. *Criterion,* 9 (April 1930), 533-35, 575-77.

In praising West's standards for criticism, Fletcher reveals his own standards.

275. ——. Rev. of *Lincoln* by Emil Ludwig. *Criterion,* 9 (July 1930), 737-39.

A harsh review. Interesting attitudes of a Southern regionalist toward the North's Civil War president are revealed.

276. ——. "Marine Eden." *This Quarter,* 2 (July-September 1930), 178-80.
Poem.

277. ——. "On Death Masks." *New Freeman,* 24 September 1930, pp. 37-38.

Essay. Death is as varied and unaccountable as life is, and suffering is not always the destiny of the evil, but the privilege of the good. Ethically and morally neither life nor death has any particular justification. The experiencing subject requires an object to experience and the relation between them lies in the plane of spiritual events, where both good and evil are necessary to each other and can be transcended only by vital experience.

278. ——. "Some Thoughts on French Painting 1910-1930." *This Quarter,* 3 (October-December 1930), 356-60.

Essay. Cursory look at the French art scene. Valuable for the poet's thought that there is not such a thing as "abstract form," only concrete form.

279.   ———. "Education Past and Present." *I'll Take My Stand: The South and the Agrarian Tradition.* By Twelve Southerners. New York: Harper, 1930. pp. 92-121.

Written for the "I'll Take My Stand Southern Symposium" which was held in order to uphold American regionalism, specifically Southern regionalism in the Agrarian tradition, as a thing to be culturally valued. This essay examines the South's contribution to education in the United States. The overall conservative tone of this essay is worthy of note.

280.   ———. "Hymn to the Present Day," "Jazz Age," "Manhattan Nights," "Demolition of the Waldorf," and "Amy Lowell." *Imagist Anthology 1930.* London: Chatto & Windus, 1930. pp. 82-96.

Poems.

281.   ———. "Introduction." *The True Travels, Adventures, and Observations of Captain John Smith, Faithfully Reprinted From the Original Edition.* ed. John Gould Fletcher. New York: Rimington and Hooper. 1930.

Essay. See also I-C-7.

282.   ———. "Gulf-Weed in Brittany." *New York Herald Tribune Books,* 25 January 1931, p. 6.

Poem.

283.   ———. "Delacroix." *Criterion,* 10 (January 1931), 264-70.

Essay. Revolves around an exhibit of Eugene Delacroix's work at the Louvre. A critical discussion of the artist and his work.

284.   ———. "Meditation on Forty-Second Street." *Nation,* 132 (15 April 1931), 415.

Poem.

285. ———. "In Tintern Valley" and "Three Fables." *The
      Island,* 1 (15 June 1931), 12, 22-24.

      Poem and short prose pieces. "The Battle of the Frogs and
      the Mice," "The Church," and "The Woodcutter." "In Tintern
      Valley" is dated Easter, 1931.

286. ———. "Building the Hudson River Bridge."
      Scribner's Magazine, 89 (June 1931), 597-98.

      Poem.

287. ———. Rev. of *Aristocracy and the Meaning of Class
      Rule* by Philipe Mairet. *Criterion,* 10 (July 1931), 757-
      69.

      Fletcher takes to task a book which has as its thesis the total
      breakdown of the Christian schema of human relationships.

288. ———. "Pablo Picasso" and "The Man Beneath
      the Mountain: A Poem." *The Island,* 1 (15 September
      1931), 36-37, 62.

      Essay and poem. Judges Picasso to be one of the least
      satisfying painters in the world. Sees strength in the black line
      designs, however judges him a failure with the brush. Accuses
      Picasso of not bringing conflicting tendencies into harmony but
      rather with simply restating tendencies as they arise. He is a
      cold blooded artist.

289. ———. Rev. of *God Without Thunder: An Orthodox
      Defense of Orthodoxy* by John Crowe Ransom and
      Prometheus and Epimethus: A Prose Epic by Carl Spitteler,
      tr. James F. Muirhead. *Criterion,* 11 (October 1931),
      127-31, 155-59.

      Outlines Ransom's thesis. He disagrees with Ransom on the
      issue of the magic process inherent in religion. He thinks it
      would have been better if Ransom had admitted "that all
      religion admits an element of magic, as well as science, insofar
      as either can be analysed by the mind. . . ." He also finds it
      difficult to accept Ransom's thesis that a myth is proportionate-
      ly valuable according to the measure of social sanction that it
      commands.

290. ———. "Woodcuts of Gwendolyn Raverat." *Print Collector's Quarterly*, 18 (October 1931), 330-350.

Essay. Views Raverat's art in the context of classicism. Her objectivism is achieved by means of directness and simplicity in its content—in essence, it is illustrative. But at the same time the state of mind induces a complexity of mood. Fletcher's insights into Raverat's work have transferability to his own imagist work.

291. ———. "Christianity and the Modern Artist" and "Poetry and the Modern Consciousness." *The Island*, 1 (15 December 1931), 101, 117-24.

Essays. "Christianity and the Modern Artist" reveals Fletcher's disillusionment with "modern" Christianity. He views it as necessary for the modern artist to accept a mystical attitude toward reality. "Poetry and the Modern Consciousness" traces the poetry scene in England and America from the mid-nineteenth century to the present. Fletcher states that the study of poetry is to study mankind at its highest moments of awareness.

292. ———. "The Battle for the Universe." *Purpose*, 3, No. 2 (1931), 72-76.

Essay. An interesting, if slight, discussion of universal truths from a historical to contemporary perspective. Fletcher's merging of religious, literary, economic, and scientific viewpoints confuses an already confusing issue.

293. ———. "Back of Beyond." *Folksay*. ed. B. A. Botkin. Norman: University of Oklahoma Press, 1931. pp. 353-46.

Poem. Comprised of "Lost Corner" and "The Farewell." Both of these poems were to be part of a yet to be published volume titled *Echoes of Arkansas*. Both are reprinted in *South Star* (1941), Section II, "Echoes of Arkansas." See I-A-24.

294. ———. "Pottery and Tiles of Bernard Beach." *Artwork*, 7, No. 26 (1931), 117-23.

Essay. Generally addresses the place of pottery in the

pantheon of the arts. The cognizance of "harmony and counterpoint of the surface and decoration playing over the melodic theme of the form, create an effect . . ." demonstrates Fletcher's solid aesthetic sensibility.

295.   ———."The Impulse of Poetry." *American Caravan IV*. ed. Van Wyck Brooks et al. New York: Macaulay, 1931. pp. 456-82.

Essay. Subscribes to Hume's axiom that "Beauty is no quality in things themselves; it exists only in the mind that contemplates them." Goes on to discuss aesthetics of various genres of art and their relation to poetry, and then philosophically addresses the same questions. This is a very important essay in the effort to come to grips with the first two decades of Fletcher's career.

296.   ———. "Elegy on an Empty Skyscraper." *Pagany*, 3 (January-March 1932), 111-13.

Poem. Reprinted in *Criterion*, 14 (April 1932), pp. 439-42, *XXIV Elegies* (1935) and *Selected Poems* (1938); also reprinted in *The History, Correspondence, and Selections from a Little Magazine, 1920-1932*. Ed. Stephen Halpert with Richard John. Boston: Beacon Press, 1969, pp. 406-08. See also I-A-21 and I-A-23.

297.   ———. "Angkor." *Theatre Arts Monthly*, 16 (May 1932), 395-96.

Poem.

298.   ———. "At the Dream's-edge Shore" and "Blue Elegy." *Poetry*, 40 (May 1932), 64-66.

Poems.

299.   ———."Death of the Gods: 363 A.D." *Theatre Arts Monthly*, 16 (September 1932), 743-46.

Poem.

300.   ———. "Three Fables." *Virginia Quarterly Review*, 9 (January 1933), 82-86.

Short prose pieces: "The Garden of Epicurus," "The Three Lookers," and "Knowall and Believeall Find the Truth."

301. ——— . "Foreward." *An Exhibition of Wood Engravings by Blair Hughes-Stanton, April 5-April 29, 1933.* London: The Zwemmer Gallery, [1933] pp. 2-3.

302. ——— . "Poet of Courage." Rev. of *The Orators: An English Study,* by W. H. Auden. *Poetry,* 42 (May 1933), 110-13.

"The fact that for the first time in human history a society has evolved which possesses no common intellectual or spiritual focus, may be the reason why the best poetry that has been produced in the last twenty years or so, often seems by comparison with the best of the past, to be shallow impulse and insufficient of technique." Considers Auden to be the most interesting English poet since World War I.

303. ——— . "Big River." *Poetry,* 42 (June 1933), 149-51.

Poem. Reprinted in *South Star* (1941). See I-A-24.

304. ——— . "Lawrence's Last Poems." Rev. of *Last Poems* by D. H. Lawrence, ed. Richard Aldington and Guiseppe Orioli. *Poetry,* 42 (June 1933), 163-65.

Views Lawrence as "an honest fanatic" as well as a great artist. States that Lawrence was too angry to be an artist in these last poems.

305. ——— . "Stephen Spender's Poems." Rev. of *Poems* by Stephen Spender. *Poetry,* 42 (July 1933), 225-28.

Fletcher marks totality of purpose as a criterion to be used in evaluating a poet. Fletcher concedes that we must allow for the possibility of a return to religion, in spite of the fatalism of the current age.

306. ——— . "American Spring." *Saturday Review of Literature,* 10 (26 August 1933), 62.

Poem.

307. ——— . "Section Versus State." Rev. of *The Influence of Sections in American History* by Frederick Jackson

Turner. *American Review*, 1 (September 1933), 483-89.

Reflects Fletcher's belief in regionalism.

308. ———. "Elegy as Epithalamium" and "Children of the Sun." *Poetry*, 43 (November 1933), 59-65.

Poems. "Elegy as Epithalamium" is reprinted in *XXIV Elegies* (1935) and *Selected Poems* (1938). See I-A-21 and I-A-23.

309. ———. "Is This the Voice of the South?" *Nation*, 137 (27 December 1933), 734-35.

Letter to the editor. Writes regarding the *Nation's* supposition that there is a miscarriage of justice transpiring in the Scottsboro case. Fletcher states that unlike Massachusetts which executed Sacco and Vanzetti (Fletcher states their innocence) for their political affiliations, the South does not persecute "Negroes" because of their politics. However, Fletcher makes it quite clear that "we" are determined to treat the Negro as a race which is largely dependent upon the white race, and is inferior to it. Fletcher believes that under this system the great majority of the race is leading happy and contented lives. Fletcher resents the fact that a Northern liberal lawyer has entered the case on behalf of the defendents, because this implies that Southern mores and justice are not capable of dealing with their own problems. He further chastises the liberal Northern press for choosing to ignore the fact that various northern cities (witness Chicago) which have faced large concentrations of Negroes after the WWI also reverted to violence and discrimination.

310. ———. "New Mexican Romance." Rev. of *The Single Glow* by Axton Clark. *Poetry*, 43 (December 1933), 165-68.

Fletcher is kind to this first book of poems by a Southwestern Imagist. This volume of poetry is a "Southwestern Number" dedicated to the memory of William Haskell Simpson. Fletcher edited the volume.

311. ———."Land of Enchantment." *Poetry*, 43 (December 1933), 150-52.

Comment. Discusses the Southwestern U. S. It attracts the poet, but does not hold him. Contemporary poets of the Southwest are more important for what they indicate than for what they have said. They have a directness and boldness of statement. (Fletcher uses the "Southwest" to mean Oklahoma, Texas, Arizona, and New Mexico.)

312. ———."Elegy on a Lost Steamship." *Latin Quarterly*, 1 (Winter 1934), 82.

Poem. c.f. "Elegy on a Lost Ship," *XXIV Elegies* (1935). See I-A-21.

313. ———."Sagebrush." *New Republic*, 78 (28 February 1934), 75.

Poem.

314. ———."Songs of the Rio Grande." *New Mexico Quarterly Review*, 4 (February 1934), 19-22.

Poem. Includes I. "Pueblo Song" and II. "Rio Grande."

315. ———."The Dilemma of Robinson Jeffers." Rev. of *Give Your Heart to the Hawks* by Robinson Jeffers. *Poetry*, 43 (March 1934), 338-42.

Predicts that Jeffers will be an important poet, but not a great poet. Sees Jeffers as being handicapped by his anti-human creed.

316. ———."Forever Upon the Prairie." *Esquire*, March 1934, p. 19.

Poem.

317. ———. Rev. of *The Boar and Shibboleth, with Other Poems* by Edward Doro. *New Republic*, 78 (18 April 1934), 291.

This review is most interesting because of Fletcher's comments on Wallace Stevens and Conrad Aiken.

318. ———. "Lytton Strachey and the French Influences on English Literature." *Books Abroad*, 8 (April 1934), 131-32.

   Essay. Attempts to put into perspective the postwar English literary scene. States that England's alliance with France during the war served to "Frenchify" English art, causing a loss of "spontaneous individuality" which it had possessed in the age of Byron, Wordsworth, Constable, and Turner. Fletcher offers an explanation for Strachey's reaction against Victorian writers and views the result as manifesting itself in the urbanity, wit, satire, logic, and nonevangelical skepticism of contemporary English art—all influenced by Strachey.

319. ———. "Deep South." *American Review*, 3 (May 1934), 244-46.

   Poems. Comprised of "The House to the Man" and "Song of Natchez Under the Hill;" both are reprinted in *South Star* (1941). "Deep South" is the heading for Section IV of *South Star*. See I-A-24.

320. ———. "Dewey's Latest Disiple [*sic*]." Rev. of *Technics and Civilization* by Lewis Mumford. *American Review*, 3 (June 1934), 392-98.

   Fletcher's distaste for the mechanistic materialism of the contemporary world is apparent. He maintains that "progress" can be included in the realm of aesthetics also.

321. ———. "Regionalism and Folkart." *Southwest Review*, 19 (July 1934), 429-34.

   Essay. Traces America's attempt to gain literary contact with itself to Van Wyck Brooks and Lewis Mumford. Views the American inventiveness as thwarted by the lack of willingness to assimilate and complete things that have been in our tradition. Sees regionalism in opposition to overindustrialized sections of the country.

322. ———. "Discovering Poetry or Discovering Revolution." Rev. of *Discovering Poetry* by Elizabeth Drew

and *Contemporary Literature and Social Revolution* by R. D. Charques. *Poetry*, 44 (July 1934), 231-35.

Charques condemns the "modernist" poet, while Drew has written a charming and disarming apology for poetry.

323. ———. "Alice Corbin's New Book." Rev. of *The Sun Turns West* by Alice Corbin. *Poetry*, 44 (August 1934), 279-82.

Interesting, if self serving, analysis of the value of anthology pieces and minor poets.

324. ———. "Elegy on London." *American Poetry Journal*, September 1934, pp. 4-6.

Poem. Reprinted in *XXIV Elegies* (1934) and *Selected Poems* (1938). See I-A-21 and I-A-23.

325. ———. "Two Travellers." Rev. of *In All Countries* by John Dos Passos and *Beyond the Mexique Bay* by Aldous Huxley. *American Review*, 3 (September 1934), 530-36.

The travel book writer is perhaps the last intellectually free specimen of writer left in the modern world.

326. ———. "Blair Hughes-Stanton." *Print Collector's Quarterly*, 21 (October 1934), 353-72.

Essay. A somewhat cursory and wide ranging review of Hughes-Stanton's art. Statements by Fletcher such as: "Our love for three-dimensional as opposed to linear form, our passion for patterns of translucent light and shade, the solid geometry of our epoch, forbids," is revelatory of the poet's views of the strictures within which he, too, must work.

327. ———. "By the Rio Grande." *Poetry*, 45 (October 1934), 23-31.

Poem. Includes "Desert," "The Dancers in the Plaza," "Nomads Song," and "Sonnets of Life, I-VII."

328. ———. "Will Take Fifty Years." *Saturday Review of Literature*, 11 (29 December 1934), 400-401.

Letter to editor. Discusses the reasons why the American public is "book-shy."

329. ———. "The Dustwhirl," and "Song of the Bufflo-Wallow." *New Republic*, 81 (December 1934), 99.
Poems.

330. ———. "The Little Reviews: Yesterday and Today." *Space*, 1 (December 1934), 84-86.
Essay. Fascinating, if superficial, analysis of the little reviews of the 1914-29 period, which he sees as predominantly left-wing and aesthetically oriented. In contrast are the "contemporary" little reviews of the depression era which are "imbued with proletarian protest." He asserts that the earlier little reviews did not focus on people, but rather on art. Art belongs to the people and is the focus of American culture. He supports cultural reawakening on a regional basis.

331. ———. "A. R. Orage: A Reminiscence." *New Democracy*, 3 (15 December 1934), 152-53.
Essay. Eulogy recounting his association with this radical writer. In his introductory paragraph Fletcher recounts that he himself had come to London to learn something about being a writer after having spent four years at Harvard and learning little. Also worthy of note is his admission that for him Nietzsche's criticism of the Christian faith, with its stress on noble vitures rather than on the virtues of slavelike humility, seemed to be final.

332. ———. "The Man Beneath the Mountain (In Memorian, D. H. Lawrence)," *American Scholar*, 4 (Winter 1935), 97-99.
Poem. Reprinted from *The Island*, 15 September 1931, p. 62.

333. ———. "A Century of Progress." Rev. of *Freedom Versus Organization* by Bertrand Russell. *American Review*, 4 (January 1935), 377-84.
Fletcher's conservative politics and economics are exhibited.

334. ———. "Kentucky Georgics." Rev. of *Man With a Bull
Tongue Plow* by Jesse Stuart. *Poetry*, 45 (January
1935), 217-20.

   Stuart's book suffers, Fletcher says, from the same defect
which made *Spoon River Anthology* almost unendurable, and
which in the end defeated Vachel Lindsay. "It is all too much in
the same key, in the same mood. . . ."

335. ———. "The Modern Southern Poets." *Westminster
Magazine*, 23 (January-March 1935), 229-51.

   Essay. Especially about Tate and Warren as well as the other
Fugitives. Fletcher asserts that Tate's craftmanship is
detrimental to his poetry. The implication is that there is an
inverse correlation between craft and emotional content.

336. ———. Rev. of *Atlantides* by Haniel Long and *Daemon
in the Rock* by Edwin Richardson Frost. *New Republic*,
81 (6 February 1935), 368-69.

   Lambasts *Daemon in the Rock*, however, is full of praise for
Atlantides. States that Long is the male American poet who has
dared to attack the theme of "sexual love."

337. ———. "American Dream." Rev. of *American Song* by
Paul Engle. *Poetry*, 45 (February 1935), 285-88.

   Some interesting remarks on the timelessness of poetry.

338. ———. "On Mesa Verde." *New Mexico Quarterly
Review*, 5 (February 1935), 3-6.

   Poem. Reprinted in *The Burning Mountain* (1946). See I-A-25.

339. ———. "Ruskin." Rev. of *John Ruskin: An Introduction to
Further Study* by R. H. Wilenski. *American Review*, 4
(February 1935), 504-12.

   A tone of kinship develops between what Fletcher perceives
to have been Ruskin's attitudes toward industrialization and
Fletcher's own attitudes toward twentieth-century industrialization.

340. ———. "Stieglitz Spoof." Rev. of *America and Alfred Stieglitz: A Collective Portrait*, ed. Waldo Frank et al. *American Review*, 4 (March 1935), 588-602.

   The last section, in which Fletcher discusses the relationship between photographer and photograph, as artist and art, is particularly good and has implications beyond photography.

341. ———. "Hymn to the New Dead," "Twentieth Century," and "Elegy on the Last Judgment." *Alcestis*, 1 (April 1935), [17-21, 24-29].

   Poems. "Elegy on the Last Judgment" is reprinted in *XXIV Elegies* (1935) and *Selected Poems* (1938); c.f. "The Last Judgment," *Parables* (1925). See I-A-21, I-A-23, and I-A-14.

342. ———. "Prometheus Steel-Bound." Rev. of *Collected Poems* and *A Hope for Poetry* by C. Day Lewis. *Saturday Review of Literature*, 11 (13 April 1935), 619.

   Sees poetry as having grown increasingly moribund since the Victorian era. Finds Lewis typically broadminded, in spite of a certain awkwardness of expression.

343. ———. "Requiem for a Twentieth Century Outlaw." *Esquire*, April 1935, p. 26.

   Poem. Reprinted in the *Burning Mountain* (1946). See I-A-25.

344. ———. "An Aesthetic Humanist." Rev. of *Concerning Beauty* by Frank Jewett Mather, Jr. *American Review*, 5 (May 1935), 238-42.

   Reveals Fletcher's thoughts on Aristotelean relationships between artist and artifact.

345. ———. "Is Folk-Art Property? 'A Reply to Philip Stevenson'." *New Mexico Quarterly Review*, 5 (May 1935), 77-80.

   Essay. Stevenson's remarks were made in *New Mexico Quarterly Review* (February 1935). Fletcher supports the theory that one can live in a world dominated by the machine without necessarily being dominated by the machine. See also II-B-86.

346.   ———. "A Stone of Stumbling." Rev. of *Lectures in America* by Gertrude Stein. *American Review*, 5 (Summer 1935), 379-84.

The modern writer has little choice, if any, in the present state of politics, ethics, economics, religion, and social life, except to be either naturalistic or romantic.

347.   ———. Rev. of *Wheels and Butterflies* by W. B. Yeats. *Southern Review*, 1 (Summer 1935), 199-203.

Fletcher attempts to place Yeats in the pantheon of twentieth-century poetry.

348.   ———. "Farewell to the Mountain." *Saturday Review of Literature*, 12 October 1935, p. 4.

Poem.

349.   ———. "Education for Living." *The Wiley Bulletin*, December 1935, p. [1-2].

Essay. Reprint of address which Fletcher had given on higher education at Norman, Oklahoma, 16 November 1935. Fletcher rhetorically asks, "What is a higher education for?" and goes on to provide his views on the subject.

350.   ———. "Gerard Manley Hopkins; Priest or Poet?" *American Review*, 6 (January 1936), 331-46.

Essay. Explores whether the dogmatism of Hopkin's Catholicism effects his poetry. Asserts that the poetry of Hopkins rests on three main lines of mental activity: 1. His feeling for God, of the awfulness and incomprehensibility of God; 2. His belief that nature both in her rich and joyous and sad and stern moods is the book in which man can best read the message of that awfulness and incomprehensibility; and 3. His sense of fundamental equality of men.

351.   ———. "Irradiations XVI" and "Steamers." *Scholastic*, 28 March 1936, p. 13.

Poems. "Irradiations" reprinted from *Irradiations, Sand and Spray* (1915), *Preludes and Symphonies* (1922 and 1930); reprinted in

Selected Poems (1938). "Steamers" reprinted from *Irradiations, Sand and Spray* and *Preludes and Symphonies* (1922 and 1930). See I-A-6, I-A-23, and I-A-13.

352. ———. "Herald of Imagism." Rev. of *Amy Lowell: A Chronicle* by S. Foster Damon. *Southern Review*, 1 (Spring 1936), 813-27.

Views the fact that Amy Lowell was a New Englander as being evident in her poetry, as well as crucial to an understanding of that poetry. Fletcher reveals that during his sojourn at Harvard he was under the illusion that the Southern culture to which he had been born was dead, and that the only culture worth noting, since the South seemed unlikely to recover its lost heritage, was that of Europe. He provides us with an intimate insight into the central councils of the Imagist movement, and, in particular, his view of his own role in the movement.

353. ———. "The Story of Arkansas." *Arkansas Gazette: State Centennial Supplement,* 15 June 1936, pp. 1-25.

Prose (history). Sometimes referred to as "The Epic of Arkansas." Reprinted in *South Star* (1941) in slightly modified form. See I-A-24.

354. ———. "The Prelude of Storm." *Saturday Review of Literature,* 15 August 1936, p. 4.

Poem. Reprinted in *Selected Poems* (1938), I-A-23.

355. ———. "Pittsburgh Epic." Rev. of *Pittsburgh Memoranda* by Haniel Long. *Saturday Review of Literature,* 22 August 1936, p. 17.

"The difference between the American poet and his cousin, the English poet, is a difference between concentration on utterance . . . Perhaps it is because here in this continent the gap between the brute facts of life and the poetic impulse itself lies deeper than elsewhere, that the American poet has so rarely found himself the ability to construct works of large scope, in which the form is appropriate to the content at every point."

356. ———. "Four Autumn Love Songs." *University
Review*, 3 (Autumn 1936), 5-7.

> Poems. "The Hour," "Song of the Midnight Rain," "To an
> Autumn Rose," and "The Gifts Demanded." "Song of the
> Midnight Rain" and "To an Autumn Rose" are reprinted in
> *Selected Poems* (1938). See I-A-23.

357. ———. "The Ozark Singer." *Criterion*, 16 (October
1936), 1-13.

> Short story.

358. ———. "Requiem for H.M." *Poetry*, 49 (December
1936), 165.

> Poem. Fletcher joins with other *Poetry* regulars in eulogizing
> Harriet Monroe, the founder of *Poetry*.

359. ———. "Preface to *Preludes and Symphonies*." *Southern
Poets*. ed. Edd Winfield Parks. New York: American
Book Company, 1936. pp. 364-67.

> This item appears in the appendix which is titled "Theories
> of Poetry by Southerners." See also I-A-13 and I-A-13-a.

360. ———. "White Symphony," "Down the Mississippi," "Earth," "The Swan," "The Black Rock," and
"The House to the Man." *Southern Poets*. ed. Edd
Winfield Parks. New York: American Book Company, 1936. pp. 249-68.

> Poems. "White Symphony" appears in *Goblins and Pagodas*
> (1916), *Preludes and Symphonies* (1930), and *Selected Poems* (1938).
> "Down the Mississippi" appears in *Breakers and Granite* (1921)
> and *Selected Poems* (1938); see also I-B-113. "Earth" is reprinted
> from *Yale Review* (July 1919), see I-B-92; "The Swan" appears in
> *The Black Rock* (1928); "The Black Rock" appears in *The Black Rock*
> (1928) and *Selected Poems* (1938), see also I-B-107; and "The House
> to the Man" appears in *South Star* (1941). See I-A-7, I-A-13,
> I-A-23, I-A-11, and I-A-16.

361. ———. "Edward Thomas." Rev. of *Edward Thomas*:

A Biography by Robert P. Eckert. *University Review*, 4 (Winter 1937), 136-37.

   A synoptic rendering of Thomas's work and life.

362. ————. "Masters and Men." Rev. of *Poems of People* by Edgar Lee Masters. *Poetry*, 49 (March 1937), 343-47.

   Sees Masters as having added realism to American poetry. "Masters, is primarily and overwhelmingly, an epic and dramatic poet."

363. ————. "Camera in a Furrow." Rev. of *Hounds on the Mountain* by James Still. *New Republic*, 91 (28 July 1937), 343.

   Poetry which springs from the direct observation of nature is not always the best kind of poetry.

364. ————. "Portrait of Edwin Arlington Robinson." *North American Review*, 244 (Autumn 1937), 24-26.

   Poem.

365. ————. "Salute to Kansas City" and "Conversation With a Midwinter Sky." *University Review*, 4 (Autumn 1937), 5-[7].

   Essay and poem. The essay "Salute to Kansas City" is reminiscence about two 1934 visits to the city. Fletcher views K.C. as a gateway to the west. "Conversation with a Midwinter Sky" is reprinted in *Selected Poems* (1938). See I-A-23.

366. ————. "Shanks Discovers Poe." Rev. of *Edgar Allan Poe* by Edward Shanks. *Poetry*, 50 (September 1937), 353-56.

   Agrees that Poe, not Baudelaire, was the first symbolist poet. Fletcher likes Poe, but not Shanks's book.

367. ————. "Arkansas Red Haw." *New Republic*, 92 (13 October 1937), 264-65.

   Poem. Reprinted in *South Star* (1941). See I-A-24.

368.   ———. "Ascent of Monadnock, I-III." *Poetry*, 51 (October 1937), 14-16.

Poem. Reprinted in *Selected Poems* (1938); c.f. "The Monadnock", *Poetry* (December 1917), I-B-62.

369.   ———. "The Reason for Regionalism: A Reply to Left Wing Critics." *American Prefaces*, 3 (December 1937), 39-41.

Essay. Fletcher believes that the preservation of distinctive regional cultures will serve to strengthen the nation's cultural fiber.

370.   ———. "Poems Written on a Tour." *University Review*, 5 (Winter 1938), [128]-131.

Poems. "Crossing the Alleghenies," "Changing Landscape," "New Salem, Illinois," "Sunset: New Salem, Illinois," and "Towards Kansas: Grasshopper Dance."

371.   ———. "Three Poems." *University Review*, 5 (Spring 1938), [159]-164.

Poems. "Symphony of the New Year," "At the Old House," and "The Three Oaks." "Symphony of the New Year" and "At the Old House" are in *Selected Poems* (1938); "The Three Oaks" is reprinted in *South Star* (1941). See I-A-23 and I-A-24.

372.   ———. "Transcontinental Tour (In Memory of a Journey from New Hampshire to Kansas City, 1937)." *University Review*, 5 (Autumn 1938), [5]-10.

Poems. "Farewell to Peterborough," "Vermont: Green Mountain Pass," "Second Day's Waking: Wellsville, New York," "Over the Prairie, Ohio," "Richmond, Indiana: The Old Hotel," "Midland Metropolis (Indianapolis)," "Ballad of a Dark Prairie," and "Kansas City."

373.   ———. "Illusion for Illusion." Rev. of *Illusion for Illusion: A Study of the Sources of Poetry* by Christopher Caudwell. *Poetry*, 53 (October 1938), 40-45.

Fletcher reacts adversely to a marxist approach to poetry.

374. ———. "Foreward" and "Requiem for a Twentieth Century Outlaw." *Muse Anthology of Poetry.* Poe Memorial Edition. New York: Carlyle Straub, 1938. pp. 14-28, 402.

Essay and poem. In his foreward Fletcher observes that Poe was in exile at home in contrast to more recent expatriates. Also provocative is Fletcher's musing that their might be reason to think that all first-rate literature is created because of some failure to adjust to the business of living—hence there is an effort by the imagination to overcome some defect. Fletcher ends his essay by focusing on Poe's influence on French writers of the nineteenth and twentieth centuries.

375. ———. "Whitman, Without and Within." Rev. of *Whitman* by Newton Arvin and *Walt Whitman and the Springs of Courage* by Haniel Long. *Poetry,* 53 (February 1939), 273-79

Fletcher's respect for Whitman's poetry is evident in this rather straightforward and substantive review.

376. ———. "Two Poems on Mark Twain." *University Review,* 5 (Summer 1939), 253-54.

Poems. "Elmira, New York: Thoughts of Mark Twain" and "Hannibal, Missouri: Mark Twain Again."

377. ———. "Recuerdos de Mexico." *New Mexico Quarterly Review,* 9 (August 1939), 135-39.

Poems. Comprised of 1. "Moctezuma," 2. "Toreadors," 3. "Chapultepec," 4. "Holy Week, Ixmiquipan," 5. "End of Dry Season," and 6. "Mexico."

378. ———. "Ant Time." *Saturday Evening Post,* 2 September 1939, p. 28.

Poem.

379. ———. "Irradiations VII," "Jade Elegy," and "Stevedores." *Scholastic,* 18 September 1939, p. 23E.

Poems. "Irradiations" has previously appeared in *Irradiations,*

Sand and Spray (1915), *Preludes and Symphonies* (1922 and 1930), and
Selected Poems (1938). "Jade Elegy" is reprinted from *XXIV Elegies*
(1935) and *Selected Poems* (1938). "Stevedores" is reprinted from
"Down the Mississippi" which has previously appeared in *Poetry*
(October 1920), see I-B-113; and in *Breakers and Granite* (1921)
and *Selected Poems* (1938). See I-A-6, I-A-13, I-A-23, I-A-21,
and I-A-11.

380. ———. "Two Plainsmen." Rev. of *Corn* by Paul
Engle and *The High Plains* by Kenneth Porter. *Poetry*,
54 (September 1939), 342-45.

Proclaims the intrinsic importance of the Great Plains to the
American culture; we learn little about them except in glimpses
from our literature. Views poetry as a steady attempt to shape
the order of hard fact into a very different order of fact
transfused by the human imagination.

381. ———. "Russia Invades Poland." *American Mercury*,
48 (December 1939), 490.

Poem.

382. ———. "Reason's Unreason." Rev. of *Collected
Poems* by Robert Graves. *Kenyon Review*, 2 (Winter
1940), 100-103.

A very negative review in which Fletcher displays some of
his wide knowledge of poetics, including Welsh metrics.

383. ———. "Deer Dance." *American Mercury*, 49 (January
1940), 107.

Poem.

384. ———. "The Ozarks." *Poetry*, 55 (February 1940),
248-49.

Poem. Reprinted in *The Burning Mountain* (1946). See I-A-25.

385. ———. "Poems of a Friar." Rev. of *Clothed With the
Sun* by Fray Angelico Chavez. *Poetry*, 55 (March
1940), 338-40.

Chavez "has retained the correct approach to poetry, by dint of living largely removed from the anti-poetic progress of the twentieth century."

386. ———. "Robert Frost the Outlander." *Mark Twain Quarterly*, Spring 1940, pp. 3-4, 23.

    Essay. Insights into Frost's relationship with Ezra Pound during Frost's years as a fledgling poet in England. Compares Frost to Thoreau in their common disdain for material values.

387. ———. "Song of the Mountain." *New Republic*, 102 (22 April 1940), 535.

    Poem.

388. ———. "Rio del Norte." *Christian Science Monitor Weekly Magazine Section*, 22 June 1940, p. 15.

    Poem.

389. ———. "Crow-Time." *American Mercury*, 50 (July 1940), 330-31.

    Poem.

390. ———. "Journey to the Pueblo." *Christian Science Monitor Weekly Magazine Section*, 3 August 1940, p. 14.

    Poem.

391. ———. "Lorca In English." Rev. of *Poems of F. Garcia Lorca, The Poet in New York and Other Poems* and *Blood Wedding* by Frederico Garcia Lorca. *Poetry*, 56 (September 1940), 343-47.

    Fletcher gives his perceptions of what is required of a translator.

392. ———. "Cricket Time." *Ladies Home Journal*, October 1940, p. 65.

    Poem.

393. ———. "Mowing Time." *New Republic*, 104 (27 January 1941), 109.

    Poem.

394. ———. "Cottonwood in Autumn" and "To a Raincloud." *New Mexico Quarterly Review*, 11 (February 1941), 107.

Poems.

395. ———. "Attitude of Youth." *Saturday Review of Literature*, 22 February 1941, p. 10.

Poem.

396. ———. "Bullfrog Time." *American Mercury*, 52 (April 1941), 426.

Poem.

397. ———. "Memorial for 1940." *Poetry*, 58 (May 1941), 65-66.

Poem.

398. ———. "Correspondence." *Poetry*, 58 (July 1941), 230-31.

Letters to the editor. Complementary of W. T. Scott's article "The Dry Reaction," *Poetry*, (May 1941). Fletcher shows his own disdain for those younger poets whom he perceives as "neo-classicists" who have been provided too many theories, theses, rules and prohibitions by academically minded teachers.

399. ———. "Three Poems." *Rotarian*, July 1941, p. 19.

Poems: "Bee Time," "Rain Time," and "Summer Time." There is also a very brief biographical blurb with a photograph of Fletcher on p. 5.

400. ———. "Squire of Gayeta Lodge." *Saturday Review of Literature*, 12 July 1941, pp. 3-4, 16.

Prose portrait. Devoted to Charles J. Finger, an Irish writer and editor of *All's Well*, living near Fayetteville, Arkansas. Fletcher says that Finger was, perhaps, the most extraordinary man he ever knew.

401. ———. "August, 1940." *Furioso*, Summer 1941, 6-9.

Poem. Reprinted in *The Burning Mountain* (1946).

402. ——. "Off the Highway." *Good Housekeeping*, October 1941, p. 46.

   Poem.

403. ——. "Shelley in 1940." *Saturday Review of Literature*, 8 November 1941, p. 12.

   Poem.

404. ——."Old South Revisited." *Yale Review*, 31 (December 1941), 334-35.

   Poem.

405. ——. "Dust Swirl Over Manhattan." Rev. of *The Dust Which is God* by William Rose Benét. *Poetry*, 59 (January 1942), 213-17.

   Fletcher is uncomplimentary in his evaluation of these poets' fulfilling the heritage upon which their styles are based. He feels that Benét's fictionalized autobiography is one of the great documents of our time. He, again blames the machine for the world's ills. He sees two different and utterly contradictory attitudes toward life as dominant: 1. "The success ethic"; and 2. An exaltation of the scholar-artist or the self-detached scientist, leading to "expression for expression's sake."

406. ——. "Stars, Fixed and Variable." Rev. of *And in the Human Heart: A Sonnet Sequence* by Conrad Aiken and *The North Star and Other Poems* by Laurence Binyon. *Poetry*, 60 (June 1942), 149-52.

   Finds Aiken immitating the Elizabethans. Binyon suffers in comparison with Aiken.

407. ——. "Deep South, 1942." *Saturday Review of Literature*, 19 September 1942, p. 17.

   Poem.

408. ——. "Flight from Egypt." *University Review*, 9 (Winter 1942), [74].

   Poem.

409. ———. ["Homage to Ford Madox Ford"]. *New Directions*. Norfolk, Conn.: New Directions, 1942. pp. 472-74.

   This issue is a festschrift for Ford. Fletcher reminisces about his early years in England and Paris and Ford.

410. ———. "The Last Time." *Furioso*, Winter 1943, p. 19.

   Poem.

411. ———. "What Has Happened to American Poetry Since 1912?" *Crescent*, Winter-Spring 1943, pp. 2-4.

   Essay. An assessment of the poetry scene since he came upon it.

412. ———. "Poems of 1942." *University Review*, 9 (Spring 1943), [162-166].

   Poems. "Poetry Readings at a Midwest Junior College," "At the Piano 1902-1942," "Journey to the Western Ozarks," "The Yellow Lily," "Mockingbird at Pea Ridge," and "The Sunflower."

413. ———. "The Poetry of Survival." Rev. of *New Poems, 1943: An Anthology of British and American Verse*, ed. Oscar Williams. *Saturday Review of Literature*, 18 September 1943, p. 25.

   An interesting review with particular chastisement of John Berryman.

414. ———. "Poems in Counterpoint." Rev. of *Four Quartets* by T. S. Eliot. *Poetry*, 63 (October 1943), 44-48.

   Fletcher praises these poems for their musicality. Finds Eliot's use of form appropriate to his subject matter. Sees Eliot remaining as an important poet only because of his craftsmanship.

415. ———. "Poems as Spur to Battle." Rev. of *War Poems*

of the United Nations, ed. Joy Davidman. *Saturday Review of Literature*, 11 December 1943, pp. 26, 28.

"Most poets had lives that involve most difficulty in adjustment to the vast mass of ignorance and common selfishness" that is man. "The poet is the type of writer most capable of sacrificing his immediate interests for the sake of some future goal which he envisages imaginatively."

416. ———. "The Burning Mountain." *University of Kansas City Review*, 10 (Spring 1944), 171-73.

Poem. Reprinted from *The Black Rock* (1928) and reprinted in *The Burning Mountain* (1946). Fletcher's translations of Ivan Goll's "Landless John Discovers the West Pole" and "Landless John the Double Man" appear on pp. 174-77; see I-C-3. Also see I-A-16 and I-A-25.

417. ———. "The Triumph Over Life." Rev. of *The Triumph of Life: Poems of Consolation for the English Speaking World*. ed. Horace Gregory. *Poetry*, 64 (May 1944), 107-10.

Deems this anthology the best which has appeared, or is likely to appear, during World War II.

418. ———. "Report on a Renaissance." Rev. of *A Vanderbilt Miscellany: 1919-1944*, ed. Richmond Croom Beatty. *Saturday Review of Literature*, 17 June 1944, pp. 17-18.

Presents some interesting Fletcherian observations concerning the role of education in the South's recovery from the Civil War. The Fugitives, or Agrarians, were confronted with the conflict between the uniform meaninglessness of an industrial age and the purposefullness of humanity dependent on deep loyalty, poetry, myth, and on a strongly rooted folk tradition.

419. ———. "Ode to New York." *Quarterly Review of Literature*, 1 (Summer 1944), 270-72.

Poem. Reprinted in *The Burning Mountain* (1946). See I-A-25.

420. ——. "Adventures in Idiom." Rev. of *Poems 1923-1943* by James Daly. *Poetry*, 64 (July 1944), 223-25.

Fletcher sees many of the contemporary poets going soft under the impact of social crisis.

421. ——. "Cutting the Trees." *Good Housekeeping*, August 1944, p. 46.

Poem.

422. ——. "Like a Sky Above Orchards." Rev. of *Eloges and Other Poems* by St. John Perse [pseud. for Alexis Saint-Legér]. *New Republic*, 111 (4 September 1944), 282.

Judges Saint-Legér's work as symbolism at its purest.

423. ——. "The Builders of the Bridge." *Crescendo*, 3 (Autumn 1944) pp. 8-9.

Poem. Reprinted in *The Burning Mountain* (1946). The poem is a homage to James Franklin Lewis. See I-A-25.

424. ——. "East Goes West in Arkansas." *Asia and the Americas*, 44 (December 1944), 538-41.

Essay. Discussion of the Japanese relocation centers located in Arkansas. Attempts a rough estimate of the potential value of some of Japanese-Americans as farmers. Presents a fine description of the bleakness of the relocation camps.

425. ——. "We Have Lost the Silk." *Maryland Quarterly*, No. 3 (1944), 132.

Poem.

426. ——. "Gentle Satirist." Rev. of *The Selected Poems: 1912-1944* by Alfred Kreymborg. *Poetry*, 66 (July 1945), 215-19.

Views poetry during the last thirty years as having moved away from the qualities of native sentiment, honest observation, and playful sympathy. Sees Kreymborg's range of expression as significantly narrow.

427. ———. "Firefly Time." *Good Housekeeping*, August
1945, p. 44.

 Poem.

428. ———. "What Price an Anthology." Rev. of *Poet to
Poet, a Treasury of Golden Criticism*, ed. Houston
Peterson and William S. Lynch. *Poetry*, 66
(September 1945), 345-48.

 Finds that this book proves that poets are seldom at their
best when discussing other poets. Fletcher's disdain is wry in
viewing poetry as escapism midst a world at war.

429. ———. "The Ablative Estate." Rev. of *Ancestor's
Brocades: The Literary Debut of Emily Dickinson* by
Millicent Todd Bingham and *Bolts of Melody: New
Poems of Emily Dickinson*, ed. Mabel Loomis Todd and
Millicent Todd Bingham. *Sewanee Review*, 53
(October-December 1945), [661]-70.

 "The truth is, that the world has no place for real
poets. . . . A poet has to live in the world, while doing
something that the world will only accept upon sufferance."

430. ———. "On a Day for Greatness (August 11-12,
Seattle to San Francisco)." *Interim*, Vol. 2, No. 1
(1945), pp. 23-25.

 Poem.

431. ———. "Orient and Contemporary Poetry." *Asian
Legacy and American Life*. ed. A. E. Christy. New York:
John Day, 1945. pp. 145-74.

 Essay. Gives the historical beginnings of the Imagist group in
1909. Points out this group's attraction to oriental poetry
genres. Discusses the effect that oriental poetical imagination
had on him and other poets. If French symbolism . . . is the
father of Imagism then Chinese poetry was its foster father. A
very important essay; necessary to the understanding of
Fletcher's poetry as well as his critical perceptions.

432. ———. "James Franklin Lewis." *Experiment*, 2 (Winter 1945-46), 95-96.

>Essay. Eulogy for Lewis.

433. ———. "On the Poetry of James Franklin Lewis." *University of Kansas City Review*, 13 (Winter 1946), 151-53.

>Essay. This issue of *UKCR* is, in effect, a festschrift for Lewis. Fletcher analyzes Lewis' use of the objective correlative.

434. ———. "A Spiritual Pilgrim." Rev. of *The Grist Mill* by Haniel Long. *Saturday Review of Literature*, 16 March 1946, p. 24.

>Fletcher sees Greek elements in Long, a fellow Southern writer. Labels Long a mystic and goes on to discuss the place of mysticism in contemporary American poetry.

435. ———. "Why No-One Trusts a Poet." Rev. of *The War Poets: An Anthology of War Poetry of the Twentieth Century*, ed. Oscar Williams. *Poetry*, 67 (March 1946), 244-49.

>States that war is a catastrophe without meaning, and because poets have realized this fact they are not likely to be listened to. The poet is entrusted with the responsibility of questioning myths. Some poets of recent years, particularly Yeats, avoided this responsibility by inventing new myths.

436. ———. "What the Dead Can Teach." *Briarcliffe Quarterly*, 3 (July 1946), 134-36.

>Poem.

437. ———. "Who Was Henley?" Rev. of *William Ernest Henley: A Study in the Counter-Decadence of the Nineties* by Jerome Hamilton Buckley. *Sewanee Review*, 54 (October-December 1946), 716-20.

>Focuses on the names and import of the English *fin de siècle*.

438. ———. "In Calvary Cemetery." *Pacific Review*, 2
(November 1946), 134-36.
  Poem.

439. ———. "One-Dimensional America." Rev. of *Brady's
Bend and Other Ballads* by Martin Keller and *No Rain
From These Clouds* by Kenneth Porter. *Poetry*, 69
(December 1946), 171-74.
  One sees Fletcher at his sarcastic best in his handling of
Keller's book.

440. ———. "Two Victorians: Trollope and Hardy." Rev.
of *The Trollopes: The Chronicles of a Writing Family* by
Lucy Poate Stebbins and Richard Poate Stebbins;
and *Thomas Hardy the Novelist: An Essay in Criticism* by
David Cecil. *Sewanee Review*, 55 (January-March
1947), 173-78.
  Dwells primarily on Hardy. However, Trollope's ac-
quiescence to the lore of commercialism is given attention.

441. ———. "The Bells at Stanford," "Fan Palm," and
"Date Palm." *Southwest Review*, 32 (Winter-Autumn
1947), 132, 344.
  Poems.

442. ———. "Poetry, 1937-1947." *Georgia Review*, 1
(Summer 1947), 153-62.
  Essay. Passes judgment on Harte Crane, William Carlos
Williams, Marianne Moore, Robinson Jeffers, T. S. Eliot, C.
Day Lewis, W. H. Auden, Robert Graves, Edith Sitwell, Louis
MacNiece, Stephen Spender, and devotes particular attention
to the Fugitives, Allen Tate, John Crowe Ransom, and Robert
Penn Warren. Also mentioned are Robert Frost, Wallace
Stevens, Stephen Vincent Benét, Karl Shapiro, and Paul Engle.
A broad but shallow critical assessment.

443. ———."Max Mayer: In Memoriam." *Arkansas Gazette*, 28 September 1947, p. 5B.

Eulogy. To the architect who had built Fletcher's home.

444. ———."Forward." *A Pepper-Pod: Classic Japanese Poems Together With Haiku* by Shōson [Kenneth Yasuda]. New York: Knopf, pp. vii-x.

Fletcher distinguishes between the Japanese haiku poet and the Western poet on the basis that the Japanese poet is content to suggest an object, and leaves the resulting emotion for the reader to complete in his own mind, whereas the Western poet states the emotion in addition to the object or objects that provoked it.

445. ———. "Mohandas Ghandhi (January 30, 1948)," "After the Storm," "At the Concert," "Inside the USA," and "The Luminous Band." *University of Kansas City Review*, 14 (Summer 1948), 255-58.

Poems.

446. ———. "Thunder in September." *Western Review*, 12 (Spring 1948), 147.

Poem.

447. ———. "Art at Eureka Springs." *Arkansas Gazette*, 30 May 1948, p. 14A.

Essay. Introduces the Art School of the Ozarks to the readers of the *Gazette*. Reflects his belief in "democratic art"—folk art.

448. ———. "History, Criticism, and the Audience." *Poetry*, 72 (May 1948), 110-12.

Correspondence. Letter to the editor in support of Karl Shapiro's assessment of contemporary poetry.

449. ———. "Room in the Highway." *Berkeley: A Journal of Modern Culture*, 1, No. 2 (1948), p. 6.

Poem.

450. ———. "Good Humor Man (Los Angeles)." *Golden Goose*, 1, No. 3 (1948), p. 12.
    Poem.

451. ———. "Sidney Lanier." *University of Kansas City Review*, 16 (Winter 1949), 97-102.
    Essay. Analysis of the technical aspects of this pioneer Southern poet. Fletcher hypothesizes on the effect which Lanier would have had on his "Symphonies" if he had read him prior to 1917.

452. ———. "Alice Corbin and Imagism." *New Mexico Quarterly Review*, 19 (Spring 1949), 47-54.
    Essay. Eulogy honoring Miss Corbin's contribution to poetry.

453. ———. "Selected Poems from a Year of Journey." *Gale*, April 1949, pp. 7-8.
    Poems.

454. ———. "Coyote in Darkness." *Arizona Quarterly*, 6 (Spring 1950), 4.
    Poem.

455. ———. "Redbud in the Ozarks." *University of Kansas City Review*, 16 (Spring 1950), 161.
    Poem.

456. ———. "A Songbag from the Ozark's Hollows and Ridgey Mountains." Rev. of *Ozark Folksongs* (Book 4) by Vance Randolph. *New York Times Book Review*, 28 May 1950, p. 7.
    Reprinted in *Missouri Historical Review* (April 1951), pp. 252-55.

457. ———. "Music Box Mountain." *Saturday Review of Literature*, 6 May 1950, p. 50.
    Poem.

458. ———. "The Ozark Folklore Society." *Arkansas Historical Quarterly*, 9 (Spring 1950), [113].

 Written in his capacity of President of the Ozark Folklore Society.

459. ———. "Some Folk-Ballads and the Background of History." Rev. of *Ozark Folksongs* by Vance Randolph. *Arkansas Historical Quarterly*, 9 (Summer 1950), [87]-98.

 Only a quasi-review. Really a historical survey of the roots of Ozark folk-ballads. Reprinted in *Missouri Historical Review* (January 1951), pp. 113-23.

460. ———. "Los Angeles Smog," and "Along the Highway, Rogers to Fayetteville." *Poetry*, 76 (July 1950), 194-96.

 Poems.

461. ———. "Palominos." *Southwest Review*, 35 (April 1950), 96.

 Poem.

462. ———. "Cottonfield in Harvest." *Southwest Review*, 35 (October 1950), 240.

 Poem.

463. ———. "Restaurants and Eating Places" and "By the Potomac." *Shenandoah*, 2 (Spring 1951), 17-19.

 Poems.

464. ———. "Posthumous Poems." *Poetry*, 84 (August 1954), 279-83.

 Poems. "Charles Baudelaire," "William Blake," "Sonnets at Sunset," and "Evening of Life."

465. ———. "Arkansas: A Look Round the Land." *A*

Southern Reader. ed. Willard Thorp. New York: Knopf, 1955, pp. 39-44.

Reprint of the first chapter of *Arkansas* (1947). See I-A-26.

466. ———. "In Poetry Man Travels." *Topic*, 2 (Spring 1962), 1-4.

Lecture. A previously unpublished lecture which had been delivered at Queens College, Cambridge University, in 1939. Reprinted in *Trace* (May 1963), pp. 1-6.

C.   Editions and Translations

1.   Faure, Élie. *The Dance Over Fire and Water*. Tr. John Gould
      Fletcher. New York: Harper, 1926.

2.   Goll, Ivan. *Jean Sans Terre/Landless John*. Tr. Lionel Abel,
      William Carlos Williams, Clark Mills, and John Gould
      Fletcher. San Francisco: Grabhorn Press, 1944.

      Poems. French and English versions of poems are on facing
      pages. Preface by Allen Tate. One hundred and seventy-five
      copies were printed.

3.   ———. "Landless John Discovers the West Pole" and
      "Landless John the Double Man." Tr. John Gould
      Fletcher. *University of Kansas City Review*, 10 (Spring
      1944), 174-77.

      Poems. Extracted from *Jean Sans Terre/Landless John;* see I-C-2.

4.   Poe, Edgar Allan. *Edgar Allan Poe*. Ed. John Gould
      Fletcher. New York: Simon and Schuster, 1926.

5.   Rousseau, Jean Jacques. *Les Rêveries du Promeneur Solitaire*.
      Tr. John Gould Fletcher. London: G. Routledge &
      Sons, Ltd. [1927].

      In his introduction to this volume Fletcher favors the doctrine
      of the superior man as an answer to modern social problems; i.e.,
      the superior man in the Confucian sense. See also I-B-248 and I-
      C-6. In the series, The Broadway Library of Seventeenth
      Century French Literature.

6.   ———. *The Reveries of a Solitary*. Tr. John Gould Fletcher.
      New York: Brentano's, 1927.

      In his introduction to this volume Fletcher favors the doctrine
      of the superior man as an answer to modern social problems; i.e.,
      the superior man in the Confucian sense; see also I-B-248 and I-
      C-5.

7.   Smith, John. *The True Travels, Adventures, and Observations of Captain John Smith, Faithfully Reprinted From the Original Edition.* Ed. and Introduction by John Gould Fletcher. New York: Rimington and Hooper, 1930.

     See also I-B-281.

D.   Miscellanea

1.   Fletcher, John Gould and Marion Bauer. "I Love the
     Night." New York: G. Schirmer, [1924]. 7 p.

     Words by Fletcher and music by Bauer. This is one of her "Four
     Poems" for high voice, Opus 16, number 2. For solo voice with
     piano accompaniment.

2.   Fletcher, John Gould. "The Second Advent (Christmas
     Greeting MCMXXVII)." [1927. 4 p.].

     Poem. Christmas issue. Woodcut by Paul Nash. Reprinted in
     The Black Rock (1928); see I-A-16. See also *Nation*, 7 December
     1927, p. 646. See also I-A-16.

3.   ———— ."For Chrismas [*sic*], 1934." [1934, n. p.].

     Poem. Christmas issue. Broadside.

4.   Fletcher, John Gould and Laurence Powell. "Arkansas
     Centennial Official Ode." [Boston]: Birchard, [1936].

     Broadside. Words by Fletcher and music by Powell. Music is in
     four-part harmony.

5.   ———— ."The Weak and Rambling One." Boston:
     Birchard, [1936].

     Words collected by Fletcher, song arranged by Powell. This
     song was taken down by dictation from the singing of Mrs.
     Dusenberry of Mena, Arkansas, in 1934. (Laurel Octavo, no.
     995).

6.   Fletcher, John Gould. "Reading His Own Poems."
     Cambridge, Mass.: Harvard Film Service, 1944.

     Recitation. Harvard Vocarium Record Series, Prof. F. C.
     Packard, Jr., editor. Side 1. "Lincoln." Side 2. "The Swan,"
     "Sunset," "Blake," and "Spring."

7.   Fletcher, John Gould and Herbert Elwell. "Lincoln."
     New York: Broadcast Music Inc., [1946].

     Piano-vocal score. Poem by Fletcher and music by Elwell.
     Requiem aeternum. Mixed chorus with baritone solo.

8. Fletcher, John Gould. "The Tree at Hirosima." [1946. n.p.].

    Poem. Christmas issue of Mr. and Mrs. John Gould Fletcher.

9. ———. "Cotton Seed Oil Mill." [1949. n.p.].

    Poem. Christmas issue. Broadside.

10. ———. "Clipper Ships." *The Library of Congress Twentieth Century Poetry in English*. Washington, D.C.: Library of Congress, 1949.

    Poem. Broadside (2 p.), "issued for distribution only with Library of Congress Poetry Record P9." Poem is prefaced with short biographical sketch of the poet; see I-D-12 for accompanying phonodiscs.

11. ———. "Clipper Ships." *Poets Reading Their Own Poems*. Washington, D.C.: Library of Congress, 1949.

    Recitation of poem. Phonodisc P9 side A and B, Twentieth Century Poets in English series, Album PII. For accompanying slip biography and text see I-D-11 above. Reissued as Phonodisc P L4 side A [1953] by Library of Congress.

II. Writing About John Gould Fletcher and His Work

A. Books

1. De Chasca, Edmund S. *John Gould Fletcher and Imagism.* Columbia, Missouri: University of Missouri Press, 1978.

   De Chasca poses and then resolves the paradox of Fletcher's being a bona fide imagist while writing poetry that was not imagistic. Part I describes Fletcher's role in the Imagist movement while paying special attention to his relationship with Amy Lowell. In Part II, a critical analysis, shows the imagistic and non-imagistic aspects of the poet's work. According to De Chasca, the Imagists were bound together by a shared vision of life, rather than by adherence to a strict doctrine.

2. Simon, Charlie May. *Johnswood.* New York: Dutton, 1953.

   A biographical reminiscence by Fletcher's wife of her life with him.

3. Stephens, Edna Buell. *John Gould Fletcher.* New York: Twayne, 1967.

   One of Twayne's United States Authors Series. A barebone, yet rather comprehensive, look at the poet's work and career. Like all books in this series, there is a profusion of quotes. One cannot help but feel that this is primarily a distillation of the author's doctoral dissertation—hence the heavy emphasis on the Oriental influences in Fletcher's work. An excellent source for a quick familiarization with Fletcher, replete with chronology.

B. Articles, Sections of Books, and Dissertations

1. Aiken, Conrad. "The Place of Imagism." *New Republic*, 3 (22 May 1915), 75-76.

   Satirizes the Imagists as a fad, and the "solemn Mr. Fletcher" who Aiken views as having produced Imagist poetry at its best in his "Irradiations." Notes that Fletcher has a good sense of rhythm, and knows how to use rhyme, although feebly at times. Finds his poetry lacking substance as is the case with the Imagists as a group. Fletcher alone seems to betray a feeling for movement, for flow and balance.

2. ———. "The Melodic Line." *Dial*, 67 (9 August 1919), 97-100.

   Essay on contemporary poetry. Focuses on H. D. and D. H. Lawrence. However, Fletcher is used as an example in a passage discussing recitative verse, as a poet who "charms and entices but does not quite enchant or take one's memory."

3. ———. *Scepticisms: Notes on Contemporary Poetry*. New York: Knopf, 1919. pp. 105-14, 187-92 and *passim*.

   Analysis of Fletcher's poetry by a fellow expatriate during the 1910-1925 period. Aiken emphasizes the subconscious element in his poetry. For all their differences, Aiken feels a kinship for his poetry.

4. ———. *Ushant, An Essay*. New York: Duell, Sloane, and Pearce, 1952. *passim*.

   Veiled reminiscences of Fletcher. Of special interest are pp. 232-39 where Aiken's narrative talks of "*farouche* John" and his illness and subsequent sojourn in Bedlam.

5. Aldrich, Ann Rochelle. "Regionalism in the Writings of John Gould Fletcher." Diss. University of Arkansas, 1975.

   Diss. Abstracts, XXXVI, 3681A. Views Fletcher as the product of a hybrid regional area—the South and the

Southwest. The poet's attitude toward the Old South was that
of an idealist and romantic. Fletcher's affiliation with the
Nashville Fugitives is also given attention as is his involvement
with the Ozark Folk Society. Ultimately, his infatuation with
the frontier and the West is examined as it manifests itself in
his work. In this context there is an excellent discussion of
Fletcher's affinity for the "hero."

6. Beaudoin, Kenneth Lawrence. "Elegy for a Southern
   Poet: John Gould Fletcher, May 12, 1950." *Prairie
   Schooner*, 24 (Summer 1950), 230.
   Poem.

7. Behrens, Ralph. "John Gould Fletcher and Rimbaud's
   'Alchimie du Verbe.' " *Comparative Literature*, 8
   (Winter 1956), 46-62.
   Discourse on Fletcher's admitted debt to Rimbaud and the
   other French symbolists. Provides textual evidence as well as
   letters to document what seems to be a valid thesis.

8. Bess, Demaree. "How Close Is War with Russia?"
   Saturday Evening Post, 24 November 1951, pp. 25, 107-
   10.
   Bess quotes (p. 109) Fletcher's *The Two Frontiers*, pointing to
   the amazing veracity of his forecasts. Offers speculation that
   Fletcher's suicide might have been a result of having his
   "brilliant analysis" of Russian-American relations ignored by
   the public.

9. Bianchi, Ruggero. "La Poetica del Secundo Imagismo:
   A. Lowell e John Gould Fletcher." *Revista de Estetica*, 9
   (1964), 214-47.
   Discusses the two poets in reference to the Imagist/
   Symbolist tradition.

10. Bodenheimer, Maxwell. "To John Gould Fletcher."
    Poetry, 54 (August 1938), 249.
    Poem. Curiously noncomplimentary.

11. Bridgewater, Patrick. "Zarathustran Images: John Gould Fletcher." *Nietzsche in Anglosaxony*. Leicester, England: Leicester University Press, 1972. pp. 173-83.

     Views Fletcher as the first important Nietzschean among American poets. Dates the Nietzschean influence to his Harvard days as a result of growing religious doubt. Nietzschean aesthetic intensity is reflected in his art, and traced in various of his books.

12. Brown, Calvin S. "The Color Symphony Before and After Gautier." *Comparative Literature*, 5 (Fall 1963), 289-309.

     An examination of the influence of Théophile Gautier upon Fletcher's experiment with color in order to elicit a certain mood.

13. Cappon, Alexander. "American Poetry." Rev. of *The Monthly Chapbook, May, 1920: "Some Contemporary American Poets"* by John Gould Fletcher. *Athenaeum*, No. 4706 (9 July 1920), 47.

     In some respects what Fletcher offers is a very good précis of Amy Lowell's *Tendencies in Modern American Poetry*. The poet's environment is viewed as having been given too much emphasis in Fletcher's symbiosis, while the poet's temperament too little.

14. ———. "An Alien Among The Imagists: John Gould Fletcher." *University Review*, 4 (Spring 1938), 165-72.

     Discusses Fletcher's philosophical and artistic differences with the Imagist group.

15. ———. "A Pulitzer Prize Poet." *University Review*, 5 (Summer 1939), 292-93.

     Alludes to "the danger" that Fletcher might have become an "aesthete." Quotes Fletcher as saying he is inspired by the senses rather than by people, seizing on the emotional essence of a scene.

16. Coffman, Stanley K. *Imagism: A Chapter from the History of Modern Poetry*. Norman: University of Oklahoma Press, 1951. pp. 175-80 and *passim*.

   A standard work on the Imagist movement. Covers Fletcher's status within, and attitude toward, the Imagist school/movement. Provides a broad overview of the Imagist poets with whom Fletcher was primarily associated during his early career. Considers Fletcher to be an Imagist and beyond.

17. ———. "John Gould Fletcher and the French Symbolists." *Books Abroad*, 24 (Autumn 1950), 364-65.

   Documents Fletcher's familiarity with French verse.

18. "Comment." *Dial*, 70 (September 1921), 376-78.

   Relates Fletcher's response, via letter to the editor, to Cowley's review of *Breakers and Granite* (*Dial*, June 1921; see II-C-x-4). Fletcher denies that Conrad Aiken had any influence at all on *Breakers and Granite*, as Cowley had suggested in his review. See also I-A-11.

19. Cowan, Louise. "The Pietas of Southern Poetry." *South: Modern Southern Literature In Its Cultural Setting*. Ed. Louis D. Rubin, Jr. and Robert D. Jacobs. New York: Doubleday, 1961. pp. 95-114.

   A brief discussion herein concerning Fletcher's chivalrousness within the context of Southern culture and modern Southern poetry.

20. Crowder, Richard. "John Gould Fletcher as Cassandra." *South Atlantic Quarterly*, 52 (January 1953), 88-92.

   Traces Fletcher's travels and career, focusing on the pessimism which the author sees as resulting from the poet's nomadic tendencies.

21. Damon, [Samuel] Foster. *Amy Lowell: A Chronicle With Extracts From Her Correspondence*. Boston: Houghton Mifflin, 1935. *passim*.

   A very important source of information regarding Fletcher's

involvement with the Imagists, particularly his relationship with Amy Lowell.

22. Darling, Oliver H. "John Gould Fletcher, Impressionist Poet: Some Aspects of His Poetry Prior to 1914." Masters thesis, Columbia University, 1951.

    One of the few evaluations of Fletcher's very early work.

23. Davidson, Donald. "In Memory of John Gould Fletcher." *Poetry*, 77 (December 1950), 154-61.

    "Opinion." An excellent short critique and biographical sketch (eulogy). The author was a friend and fellow Southern poet. Reprinted in *Still Rebels, Still Yankees and Other Essays*. Baton Rouge: Louisiana State University Press, 1957. pp. 31-40.

24. Dembo, L. S. *Conceptions of Reality in Modern American Poetry*. Berkeley: University of California Press, 1966. pp. 15-25.

    Finds Fletcher representing the Imagist "sensibility" in its most mystical form. The crux of his poetics is seen to be a theory of empathy which ends in a vision of "interpenetration." There are some very interesting parallels between Fletcher and Hart Crane.

25. Douglass, Thomas Ernest. "The Correspondence of John Gould Fletcher: A Catalogue." Diss. University of Arkansas, 1965.

    A valuable guide to the John Gould Fletcher Collection at the University of Arkansas. Fletcher donated his papers to the University Library. Consequently, the University of Arkansas has become a center for Fletcher studies. See also II-B-54 and II-B-71.

26. Emerson, Dorothy. "Poetry Corner." *Scholastic*, 28 March 1936, p. 13.

    Short biographical sketch of Fletcher and his work. "Irradiation XVI" and "Steamers" are given as examples of his work. A photograph of Fletcher is included.

27. Fairchild, Hoxie Neale. *Religious Trends in English Poetry*. New York: Columbia University Press, 1962. V, pp. [486]-93.

> Claims that Fletcher never ceased being an adolescent. This point of view is supported with biographical data. Relates this argument to his work using Fletcher's temperament as a focus for absolutist tendencies. In addition to this most provocative thesis, Fairchild examines the religious fiber of Fletcher's poetry. Her observation that Fletcher was horrified by the Old Testament as a child, and too secure economically and physically to be moved by the New Testament is most interesting.

28. "Fletcher, John Gould." *Chapbook*, June 1929, p. 16.

> "A Bibliography of Modern Poetry." Terms Fletcher "An American of considerable interest who has come to live in England."

29. Gould, Jean. *Amy: The World of Amy Lowell and the Imagist Movement*. New York: Dodd, Mead, 1975. *passim*.

> Places Fletcher within the context of the Imagist movement. Speaks disparagingly of him, alluding to his "neurotic and paranoid" tendencies.

30. Greenslet, Ferris. "The Poetry of John Gould Fletcher." *Egoist*, 2 (1 May 1915), 73.

> Sees Fletcher as stirring the reader with a sense of being.

31. Gregory, Horace and Marya Zaturenska. *A History of American Poetry, 1900-1940*. New York: Harcourt, Brace, 1946. pp. 201-16 and *passim*.

> Sympathetic evaluation of Fletcher and his poetry by two contemporary poets.

32. Harmer, J. B. *Victory in Limbo: Imagism 1908-1917*. New York: St. Martin's Press, 1975, pp. 94-99 and *passim*.

> Presents Imagism as a movement and school, placing it in the continuum of contemporary letters. Fletcher is inadvertently placed in these contexts.

33. Haun, Eugene. "Of Broken Effort and Desire: A General Consideration of the Poetry of John Gould Fletcher." *Shenandoah*, 2 (Spring 1951), [3]-16.

> This essay focuses on Fletcher's inability to objectively evaluate his own work. Fletcher is seen as a major poet who was unable to carry out a major poetic effort. Much is made out of his belief that life was essentially tragic and man is forever doomed. The poet's concentration on mood and manner are seen as compensation for a chronic lack of form. Haun implies that Fletcher's return home from Europe had an element of prodigality in it.

34. Hoffman, Frederick J., Charles Allen, and Carolyn F. Ulrich. *The Little Magazine: A History and a Bibliography*. Princeton: Princeton University Press, 1946. *passim*.

> Informative as to the nature of the many little magazines in which Fletcher published so much of his work.

35. Holmes, John A. "John Gould Fletcher." *American Poetry Journal*, September 1934, pp. 2-3.

> Focuses on Fletcher's rebelliousness and his spiritual need to live in an older civilization. Introduces "Elegy on London"; see *American Poetry Journal*, September 1934, pp. 4-6; I-B-324.

36. Hudgins, Mary D. "Composer Laurence Powell in Arkansas." *Arkansas Historical Quarterly*, 31 (Summer 1972), [182]-88.

> Recounts (p. 186) Powell's collaboration with Fletcher on the Arkansas "Centennial Ode."

37. Hughes, Glenn. *Imagism and the Imagists: A Study in Modern Poetry*. 1931; rpt. New York: Humanities Press, 1960. pp. 125-52 and *passim*.

> One of the standard authoritative works on the Imagist movement. Provides a fairly comprehensive insight into the poet, his life and his work, especially within the context of his early career.

38. "J. G. Fletcher, Poet, Found Dead in Pool." *New York Times*, 11 May 1950, p. 4F.

"Coroner Howard A. Dishough listed the death as suicide by drowning." The obituary goes on to review Fletcher's career.

39. "John Gould Fletcher." *New York Times*, 2 May 1939, p. 20E.

A brief overview of Fletcher's career, in honor of his winning of the Pulitzer Prize. Mentions that he has lived in Europe on income which had been left to him by his father. Also notes that in his writing Fletcher sought to combine poetry, painting, and music in a fused art form.

40. "John Gould Fletcher." *The Library of Congress Twentieth Century in English*. Washington, D. C.: Library of Congress, 1949.

Broadside, "issued for distribution only with Library of Congress Poetry Record P9." Prefaces poem, "Clipper Ships"; see I-D-11 and I-D-12. Mentions Fletcher's education at Philips Andover and Harvard, and goes on to give chronology of his literary career.

41. "John Gould Fletcher, 1886-1950." *Arkansas Folklore*, 1 (July 1950), 2-6.

Eulogistic enumeration of his contributions to the study of Arkansas folklore.

42. Jones, Llewellyn."Art and Life—Again." *Freeman*, 3 (27 July 1921), 473-74.

A response to Fletcher's article "Art and Life," *Freeman*, 1 (25 May 1921), p. 247; see I-B-131.

43. ———. "Flecker's Theory of Poetry." *Freeman*, 2 (22 December 1920), 354.

"Letter to editor." Comments on Fletcher's review "The Work of J. C. Squire," *Freeman*, 2 (1 December 1920), pp. 284-85; see I-B-116.

44. Kimpel, Ben. "John Gould Fletcher in Retrospect." Rev. of *Johnswood* by Charlie May Simon. *Poetry*, 84 (August 1954), 284-96.

An evaluative critique of Fletcher's career. Considers "Mexican

Quarter" his best poem. Draws attention to the fact that Fletcher
was at variance with the Imagist school. Fletcher is quoted as
saying that he never was interested in reproducing an image as an
emotion. A biographical outline is included.

45. Kreymborg, Alfred. *A History of American Poetry: Our
     Singing Strength*. New York: Tudor, 1934. *passim.*

     An evaluation of Fletcher as an individual and a poet.

46. ———. *A Troubadour: An Autobiography.* New York:
     Liveright, 1925. p. 395.

     Brief, but perceptive insight into Fletcher's sensitivity and
     loneliness.

47. Loving, Pierre. "Towards Walt Whitman." *Double
     Dealer*, 4 (September 1922), 139-42.

     Discusses various modern poets, Fletcher among them, in the
     context of having been influenced by Whitman.

48. Lowell, Amy. "The Imagists: H. D. and John Gould
     Fletcher." *Tendencies in Modern American Poetry*.New
     York: Macmillan, 1917. pp. 233-343.

     Enthusiastic praise for Fletcher as an Imagist, by the high
     priestess of the movement.

49. Lucchese, R. "John Gould Fletcher." *La Fiera Letteraria*,
     22 October 1950, p. 5.

     Eulogistic overview of Fletcher's career.

50. Lund, Mary Graham. "John Gould Fletcher: An
     Anachronism." *Southwest Review*, 51 (Winter 1966), 37-
     45.

     Interesting insights into Fletcher's belief in a universal culture,
     his relationship with James Franklin Lewis, his admiration for
     Hart Crane, and his devotion to young aspiring poets.

51. ———. "John Gould Fletcher: Geographer of the
     Uncharted Province of Beauty." *Sewanee Review*, 76
     (Winter 1968), [76]-89.

     A book by book analysis of Fletcher's aesthetic development.

52. ———. "The Love Songs of John Gould Fletcher."
Midwest Quarterly, 7 (Autumn 1965), 83-91.

> Analysis of one of the genres within the Fletcher canon.
> Focuses on the erotic imagery and marriage songs.

53. Martin, Wallace. " 'The Forgotten School of 1909' and
Origins of Imagism." *A Catalogue of Imagist Poets*. New
York: J. Howard Wotner, 1966. pp. 7-38.

> Mentions Fletcher's assessment that the art of the period
> influenced his own development (p. 16). Very brief on Fletcher *per
> se* but sets the milieu in which he functioned.

54. Moffet, James M. "A Name, Works, and Subject Index
of the Correspondence of John Gould Fletcher for
Correspondents 'L' Through 'Z'." Diss. University of
Arkansas, 1968.

> Diss. Abstracts, XXIX, 268A. See also II-B-71, for 'A' through
> 'K'.

55. Monro, Harold. "The Imagists Discussed." *Egoist*, 2
(May 1915), 77-80.

> The Imagists, including Fletcher, are discussed in a historical
> context.

56. Monroe, Harriet. "John Gould Fletcher." *Poetry*, 27
(January 1926), 206-10.

> "Comment." States that Fletcher has a subtle metaphysical
> mind. A rather cursory review of his major work to date.

57. M[onroe], H[arriet]. "On the Great River." *Poetry*, 46
(August 1935), 268-74.

> "Comment." Reflections on the Mississippi River as a central
> image in American literature. Notes that Fletcher, in "Embarka-
> tion," provides modern testimony that it still "may be loved for
> itself and sung for its glory."

58. Monroe, Harriet. *Poets and Their Art.* New York: Macmillan, 1926. pp. 87-91.

    A sympathetic gloss of Fletcher's art. Miss Monroe was an early supporter of Fletcher's poetry, publishing his first poem to be published in America.

59. ———. *A Poet's Life: Seventy Years In a Changing World.* New York: Macmillan, 1938. *passim.*

    Miss Monroe's autobiography has some interesting reminiscences about Fletcher, along with passages from his letters to her.

60. Mullins, Eustice. *This Difficult Individual: Ezra Pound.* New York: Fleet, 1961. pp. 79-82.

    Some particularly interesting insights into Fletcher's temperament. Also, relates that Fletcher's suicide was by drowning.

61. Norman, Charles. *Ezra Pound.* New York: Macmillan, 1960. *passim.*

    Elucidates Fletcher's early relationship with Pound as well as the subsequent disintegration of that relationship.

62. Nyren, Dorothy, ed. "John Gould Fletcher." *A Library of Literary Criticism: Modern American Literature.* New York: F. Ungar, 1960. pp. 190-92.

    Eleven abstracts of critical essays or reviews devoted to Fletcher's work, spanning the period 1919-1953.

63. O'Conor, Norreys J. "Impressions of John Gould Fletcher." *Southwest Review*, 38 (Summer 1953), 238-43.

    Personal recollections of Fletcher's residence in London.

64. Osborne, William R. "The Poetry of John Gould Fletcher: A Critical Analysis." Diss. Peabody College, 1955.

    Diss. Abstracts, XVI, 122. Considers Fletcher to have written and thought on opposite planes.

65. Parks, Edd Winfield. "Introduction." *Southern Poets*. New
York: American Book Company, 1936. pp. lxxx–
lxxxii, cxxii–cxxiii.

   Mentions Fletcher in the context of contemporary Southern
   poetry, in roles as cosmopolitan and traditionalist.

66. ———. *Segments of Southern Thought*. Athens: University
of Georgia Press, 1938. pp. 72-74, 113-14.

   Speaks very flatteringly of Fletcher as an innovator,
   particularly his "allusive method" and symphonies. Considers
   him in tandem with Conrad Aiken and quotes Aiken's
   judgment of Fletcher.

67. Pattee, Fred Lewis. *The New American Literature: 1890-
1930*. New York: Appleton-Century, 1937. *passim*.

   Mentions Fletcher in the context of the poetry renaissance of
   1910-1920. Not much of substance about Fletcher. He is,
   however, placed within the literary scene of the period. What is
   important is that Pattee, an important force in the study of
   American Literature in the university, finds Fletcher worthy of
   note.

68. Pearson, Norman Holmes. "The John Gould Fletcher
Collection." *Yale Library Gazette*, 30 (January 1956),
120-25.

   Sees Fletcher's life in an interesting light, as a symbol of the
   artist of our time—uneasy, troubled, yet marked with
   achievement. Presents important biographical background.
   Ostensibly this article is about the Fletcher collection at Yale
   which was donated by Pearson. Most interesting, however, are the
   quotation of marginalia and other unpublished material from the
   collection. One perceives the intense discontent which Fletcher
   experienced.

69. Pender, R. Herdman. "John Gould Fletcher." *Egoist*, 3
(November 1916), 173-74.

   Suggests that Fletcher is fundamentally a "rhythmist" rather
   than Imagist. Considers him more important for his technical
   pioneering than for the quality of his poetry.

70. Perkins, David. *A History of Modern Poetry: From the 1890's to Pound, Eliot, and Yeats.* Cambridge: Harvard University Press, 1976, pp. 341-43.

 Straight historical perspective, especially within the context of Imagism.

71. Peters, Oliver Leon. "A Name, Works, and Selected Subjects Index of the Correspondence of John Gould Fletcher for Correspondents 'A' Through 'K'." Diss. University of Arkansas, 1965.

 Diss. Abstracts, XXVI, 1048. See also II-B-54, for 'L' through 'Z'.

72. Phelps, William Lyon. "May I Suggest . . ." *Rotarian,* July 1939, pp. 48-50.

 A review of the 1938 Pulitzer Prizes. There is a passing reference to an unfamiliarity with Fletcher's work. This is notable considering that Phelps was one of the foremost scholars and academicians of the day. A photograph of Fletcher is included.

73. Pound, Ezra. "An Open Letter to John Gould Fletcher." *Poetry,* 43 (February 1943), 292.

 Takes issue with Fletcher's categorization of him in his review of Clark's *The Single Glow, Poetry,* December 1933; "I have never been a waste-lander, I am not going to issue from a place where I ain't by a path that I don't believe in. . . ."

74. Pratt, William, ed. "In Pursuit of the Fugitives." *The Fugitive Poets: Modern Southern Poetry in Perspective.* New York: Dutton, 1965. pp. 14-15.

 "Introduction." Points out that Fletcher was the only poet who had been both Imagist, expatriate, and Southerner, thereby giving him better perspective on what the Fugitives were about. Briefly discusses Fletcher's important essay "Two Elements in Poetry"; see *Saturday Review of Literature,* 27 August 1927, pp. 65-66, I-B-241.

75. Pratt, William C. "John Gould Fletcher (1886-1950)." *A Bibliographical Guide to the Study of Southern Literature*. ed. Louis D. Rubin, Jr. Baton Rouge: Louisiana State University Press, 1969. pp. 197-98.

    A very cursory bibliography, unannotated.

76. "Pulitzer Prize Winners." *Saturday Review of Literature*, 6 May 1939, p. 6.

    A short biographical sketch of Fletcher and photograph are included with those of other Pulitzer winners of the year.

77. Rock, Virginia. "The Twelve Southerners: Biographical Essays." *I'll Take My Stand, By Twelve Southerners: The South and the Agrarian Tradition*. New York: Harper and Row, 1962. pp. 365-67.

    A brief biographical sketch which astutely points out the paradoxical nature of Fletcher's career as experimenter turned traditionalist. Also discusses his suicide. Pp. 92-121 are a reprint of "Education, Past and Present" as it appeared in the 1930 edition of *I'll Take My Stand*. See I-B-279.

78. Simon, Charlie May. "John Gould Fletcher." *Lays of the New Land: Stories of Some American Poets*. New York: Dutton, 1943. pp. 211-27.

    A saccharine anecdotal biographical gloss of Fletcher by his wife.

79. Stephens, Edna Buell. "The Oriental Influence in John Gould Fletcher." Diss. University of Arkansas, 1961.

    Diss. Abstracts, XXII, 264. Follows the Oriental influence and imagery through the entire Fletcher canon. This is the most comprehensive study of this aspect of Fletcher's work to date.

80. Taupin, René. *L'Influence du Symbolisme Francaise sur la Poésie Américaine (de 1910 à 1920)*. Paris: H. Champion, 1929. *passim*.

    Discusses the influence of the French symbolists on the twentieth-century American poets—Fletcher included.

81. "University of Arkansas Library Gets John Gould
    Fletcher Library." *Arkansas Alumnus*, 6 (December
    1952), 10.

    The announcement of the University Library's acquisition of
    Fletcher's personal library. There is a description of the library in
    nonbibliographic terms.

82. Untermeyer, Louis. *American Poetry since 1900*. New
    York: Holt, 1923. pp. 316-22 and *passim*.

    Views Fletcher's later poetry as possessing greater emotional
    vitality than his earlier work. Much of what Untermeyer says
    here merely echoes what was said in *The New Era in American Poetry*;
    see II-B-83.

83. ———. *The New Era in American Poetry*. New York: Holt,
    1919. pp. 301-07.

    Presents excerpts from some Fletcher poems in order to
    support a shallow, rather unsympathetic critical discussion of the
    poet.

84. Warren, R[obert] P[enn]. "A Note on Three Southern
    Poets." *Poetry*, 10 (May 1932), 103-13.

    Objects to the omission of Fletcher from Addison Hibbard's
    anthology, *The Lyric South*. Warren makes a strong case for
    Fletcher being considered a Southern poet. In addition, he sees
    Fletcher's work as important for its extension of rhythmical
    potentials of the language.

85. Williams, Ellen. *Harriet Monroe and The Poetry Renaissance:
    The First Ten Years of Poetry*. Urbana: University of
    Illinois Press, 1977. pp. 198-202 and *passim*.

    Interesting discussion of Fletcher's relationship with Monroe—
    "not one of her confidants." Fletcher's suggestion that *Poetry* cease
    publishing new poets and concentrate on the established ones is
    most revealing.

86. Wynn, Dudley. "Antidote and Paradox." *New Mexico
    Quarterly Review* (May 1935), 81-83.

    Comment. Takes Fletcher to task for his "Reply to Philip

Stevenson," pp. 77-80 of this same issue of *New Mexico Quarterly Review;* see I-B-345.

87. Yarnell, D. A. "John Gould Fletcher." *University Review,* 2 (Winter 1936), 110-13.

Biographical and critical sketch of Fletcher's career to date. Notes that in his earlier years Fletcher wanted to be a painter and that he had studied water color. Yarnell's relation of Fletcher's reputation for grasp of detail, "a painter's gift of grasping all details," is seen as being partly responsible for leading him to Imagism. Also of particular interest is the revelation that Fletcher as a precocious child had begun to read Latin and German at age seven, reading Goethe and Schiller at an early age. Early childhood favorites were Poe and Coleridge and remained such until replaced by Whitman, Shelley, Blake, and the French symbolists. Yarnell goes on to discuss the evolution of Fletcher's poetry and his artistic evolution, particularly in the context of his relationship with Amy Lowell.

88. Yasuda, Kenneth. *The Japanese Haiku: Its Essential Nature, History, and Possibilities in English, with Selected Examples.* Rutland, Vt.: Charles E. Tuttle, 1957. pp. xvii, 9, 65, 170, 179.

Discusses Fletcher's and the Imagists' basic understanding and misunderstanding of Japanese poetry and the effect their perceptions and misperceptions has had on English poetry.

89. "The Yearling and Other Books Win Pulitzer Prizes." *Publisher's Weekly,* 135 (6 May 1939), 1684-86.

Cursory article on books winning Pulitzer Prizes, Fletcher's *Selected Poems* included. There is a photograph of Fletcher.

90. Zur, Bernard Philip. "John Gould Fletcher, Poet: Theory and Practice." Diss. Northwestern University, 1958.

Diss. Abstracts, XIX, 2605. A detailed study of the symbolist influences as well as other far ranging influences.

C. Book Reviews

i. The Book of Nature

1. Thomas, Edward. "Poems by John Gould Fletcher." Rev. of *The Book of Nature; The Dominant City: 1911-1912; Fool's Gold; Fire and Wine;* and *Visions of the Evening* by John Gould Fletcher. *Poetry and Drama,* 1 (September 1913), 363-65.

   Unimpressed by *The Book of Nature.* Views it as reflective of the poet's literary ambition.

2. "The Works of John Gould Fletcher." Rev. of *Fool's Gold; The Dominant City; Visions of the Evening;* and *The Book of Nature* by John Gould Fletcher. *Poetry Review,* 3 (August 1913), 109.

   Fletcher suffers from a need to confess all of the soul's vicissitudes with depressing results. Finds Fletcher preoccupied with the sinister aspect of things.

ii. The Dominant City: 1911-1912

1. P[ound], E[zra]. Rev. of *The Dominant City: 1911-1912* and *Fool's Gold* by John Gould Fletcher. *New Freewoman,* 1 (15 September 1913), 131-32.

   The book is seen to have a unity and a distinctive music as well as abundant imagery without hackneyed cadence.

2. ———. "Peals of Iron." Rev. of *Fire and Wine* and *The Dominant City: 1911-1912* by John Gould Fletcher. *Poetry,* 3 (December 1913), 111-13.

   Some interesting comments regarding the need for an American serious about poetry to leave the United States. Berates Fletcher's English because he is trying to use contemporary speech, and further accuses him of falling into the use of abstraction and rhetoric. At his best Fletcher is seen as being "concrete, grim, and specific."

3. Thomas, Edward. "Poems of John Gould Fletcher." Rev.
   of *The Book of Nature; The Dominant City: 1911-1912;
   Fool's Gold; Fire and Wine;* and *Visions of the Evening* by
   John Gould Fletcher. *Poetry and Drama,* 1 (September
   1913), 363-65.

   > *The Dominant City* is seen as being Fletcher's best 1913 book.
   > It is viewed as an effort to present visible London, together with
   > its effect on the poet's spirit. The book is judged to be artistically
   > true and pleasant—the total effect being of a sinister,
   > multitudinous confusion.

4. "The Works of John Gould Fletcher." Rev. of *Fool's Gold;
   The Dominant City; Visions of the Evening;* and *The Book of
   Nature* by John Gould Fletcher. *Poetry Review,* 3 (August
   1913), 109.

   > For summary see II-C-i-2.

iii. Fire and Wine

1. P[ound], E[zra]. "Peals of Iron." Rev. of *Fire and Wine* and
   The Dominant City: 1911-1912 by John Gould Fletcher.
   Poetry, 3 (December 1913), 111-13.

   > For summary see II-C-ii-2.

2. Rev. of *Fire and Wine* by John Gould Fletcher. *London Times
   Literary Supplement,* 29 May 1913, 235.

   > Finds the volume "tired," unjustified in that Fletcher is unable
   > to translate his feelings into beauty.

3. Thomas, Edward. "Poems of John Gould Fletcher." Rev.
   of *The Book of Nature; The Dominant City: 1911-1912;
   Fool's Gold; Fire and Wine;* and *Visions of the Evening* by
   John Gould Fletcher. *Poetry and Drama,* 1 (September
   1913), 363-65.

   > Not impressed with *Fire and Wine.* Views this book as being
   > representative of the author's literary ambition.

iv. Fool's Gold

1. P[ound], E[zra]. Rev. of *The Dominant City: 1911-1912* and
   Fool's Gold by John Gould Fletcher. *New Freewoman*, 1 (15
   September 1913), 131-32.

   The book has a distinctive music while avoiding hackneyed
   cadences. The tone is sustained throughout with abundant
   imagery.

2. Thomas, Edward. "Poems by John Gould Fletcher." Rev.
   of *The Book of Nature; The Dominant City: 1911-1912; Fire
   and Wine; Fool's Gold;* and *Visions of the Evening* by John
   Gould Fletcher. *Poetry and Drama,* 1 (September 1913),
   363-65.

   Not impressed by *Fool's Gold*. Views the book as reflective of the
   author's literary ambition.

3. "The Works of John Gould Fletcher." Rev. of *Fool's Gold;
   The Dominant City; Visions of the Evening;* and *The Book of
   Nature* by John Gould Fletcher. *Poetry Review,* 3 (August
   1913), 109.

   For summary see II-C-i-2.

v. Visions of the Evening

1. Thomas, Edward. "Poems of John Gould Fletcher." Rev.
   of *The Book of Nature; The Dominant City: 1911-1912; Fire
   and Wine; Fool's Gold;* and *Visions of the Evening* by John
   Gould Fletcher. *Poetry and Drama,* 1 (September 1913),
   363-65.

   Not impressed by *Visions of the Evening*. Views this volume as
   reflective of the author's literary ambition.

2. "The Works of John Gould Fletcher." Rev. of *Fool's Gold;
   The Dominant City; Visions of the Evening;* and *The Book of
   Nature* by John Gould Fletcher. *Poetry Review,* 3 (August
   1913), 109.

   For summary see II-C-i-2.

vi. Irradiations Sand and Spray

1. Aiken, Conrad. "Imagism or Myopia." Rev. of *Irradiations Sand and Spray* by John Gould Fletcher and *Some Imagist Poets: An Anthology*. *Poetry Journal*, 3 (July 1915), 233-41.

     Sees Fletcher's book as being "white hot" in its "supercilious contumacy."

2. Alden, Raymond M. "Recent Poetry." Rev. of *Irradiations Sand and Spray* by John Gould Fletcher. *Dial*, 59 (24 June 1915), 26-30.

     Thinks very little of Fletcher's Imagist theory. Finds the preface to be full of misstatements. Six other books are also reviewed; see pp. 27-28.

3. B., W. S. "The Vitality of Imagism." Rev. of *Irradiations Sand and Spray* by John Gould Fletcher. *Boston Evening Transcript*, 16 June 1915, p. 4 [part 3].

     Views the book as an example of Fletcher's belief that poetry is capable of as many gradations in cadence as music is of tune. The volume is full of subtle moods and images. The reviewer finds *Irradiations Sand and Spray* to be a sterling example of the achievement of the Imagist poets.

4. Dawson, Mitchell. Rev. of *Irradiations Sand and Spray* by John Gould Fletcher. *Little Review*, 2 (August 1915), 43-44.

     Fletcher shows considerable diversity, but does not display the usual contortions of love, hate, grief, and fear. The poet has the power of conveying a mood in terms of nature without intruding himself upon the reader.

5. Firkins, O. W. "The New Movement in Poetry." Rev. of *Irradiations Sand and Spray* by John Gould Fletcher. *Nation*, 101 (14 October 1915), 458.

     Primarily a critical article on Imagism as a movement, with the view that the Imagists' misadventure lies in the fact that in extending deviation they have annihilated the basis for defined expectation. Passing review is given to Fletcher in the last section of this essay.

6. H[enderson], A[lice] C[orbin]. Rev. of *Irradiations Sand and Spray* by John Gould Fletcher. *Poetry*, 7 (October 1915), 44-47.

   Fletcher is viewed as exhibiting a keen sensitivity to impressions, though there is a tendency for him to be too verbose, piling impression upon impression.

7. Howells, William Dean. "Editor's Easy Chair." Rev. of *Irradiations Sand and Spray* by John Gould Fletcher. *Harper's Monthly*, 131 (September 1915), 634-47.

   Views Fletcher's *vers libre* as being of a polemic flavor, consequently not very convincing. Imagist poetry is prose which has undergone a shredding process; see p. 637.

8. Lowell, Amy. "Mr. Fletcher's Verse." Rev. of *Irradiations Sand and Spray* by John Gould Fletcher. *New Republic*, 3 (15 May 1915), 48-49.

   Finds Fletcher's poems to have a remarkable fertility, vigor, and an organic quality about them. Notes that the poet's observation is very minute and exact. The book is dedicated to her.

9. Rev. of *Irradiations Sand and Spray* by John Gould Fletcher. *London Times Literary Supplement*, 22 July 1915, 247.

   The reviewer is offended by the preface which views English poetry as backward—it can only be rescued by American verse. Views Fletcher's *vers libre* as disjointed pronouncements.

10. Rev. of *Irradiations Sand and Spray* by John Gould Fletcher. *Springfield Republican*, 15 July 1915, p. 5.

11. "Verse in Variety." Rev. of *Irradiations Sand and Spray* by John Gould Fletcher. *Saturday Review of Politics, Literature, Science and Art*, 120 (28 August 1915), 211.

    Finds the Imagists revelling in prefaces. Three other books are reviewed in addition to *Irradiations Sand and Spray*.

vii. Goblins and Pagodas

1. B., W. "Modern Poetry." Rev. of *Goblins and Pagodas* and

The Tree of Life by John Gould Fletcher. *Saturday Review of Politics, Literature, Science and Art*, 126 (9 November 1918), 1039-40.

> The book is the work of a painter building a fanciful world out of his own imagination linked with reality. Finds the modernity of Fletcher's work arresting. An experiment in an attempt to express emotion in terms of the certain color which the poet believes inseparable from each mood.

2. B., W. S. "A Poetic Apostle of Goblins and Pagodas." Rev. of *Goblins and Pagodas* by John Gould Fletcher. *Boston Evening Transcript*, 17 May 1916, p. 5.

> Compliments the quality of the preface in which the poet's theory is explained, but wonders if the poems can stand by themselves. Judges that the beauty and power of the poems augment their form.

3. "The Battle Between Rhyme and Imagism." Rev. of *Goblins and Pagodas* by John Gould Fletcher. *New York Times Book Review*, 4 February 1917, p. 37.

> Considers that in spite of Fletcher's association with the Imagist movement, he is not a slave of formula. However, it is lamentable that he has deserted rhyme in his craft. Three other books, by H. D. and D. H. Lawrence, as well as the Imagist Anthology, are also reviewed.

4. D[oolittle], H[ilda]. "Goblins and Pagodas." Rev. of *Goblins and Pagodas* by John Gould Fletcher. *Egoist*, 3 (December 1916), 183-84.

> An appreciative review from a fellow Imagist.

5. Dudley, Dorothy. "Poet and Theorist." Rev. of *Goblins and Pagodas* by John Gould Fletcher. *Poetry*, 9 (October 1916), 43-47.

> Finds "Ghosts of an Old House" to be successful in spite of an occasional lack of taste and clumsiness. The symphonies are not viewed to be adequately controlled—they are founded in abstraction.

6. Firkins, O. W. "Meteorites in Verse." Rev. of *Goblins and Pagodas* by John Gould Fletcher. *Nation*, 104 (11 January 1917), 43-45.

   Five other books are reviewed in addition to *Goblins and Pagodas*. . It is seen as confirming the creed of the Imagists. Firkins is disturbed by what he perceives as a lack of form in the poetry of the Imagists.

7. "The Imagist Fog—'Goblins and Pagodas'." Rev. of *Goblins and Pagodas* by John Gould Fletcher. *Springfield Republican*, 7 January 1917, p. 15.

   A completely negative response to the symphonies. The reviewer finds neither instruction, pleasure, nor meaning in them.

8. Mencken, H. L. Rev. of *Goblins and Pagodas* by John Gould Fletcher. *Smart Set*, 51 (February 1917), 400.

   On the basis of the various volumes of poetry reviewed here, Mencken sees the Imagists "petering out." Finds Fletcher starved for effects. The color symphonies are somewhat more successful because a picture takes form from the brilliant detail and worthy earnestness. Finds the preface interesting, ideas often erroneous, but nevertheless, "not unsane."

9. W[yatt], E[dith]. "Faery-lands Forlorn." Rev. of *Goblins and Pagodas* by John Gould Fletcher. *New Republic (Fall Literary Review)*, 18 November 1916, p. 11.

   Wyatt likes the poems, but considers the preface a "pedantic rubble heap." Both the preface and the symphonies are too much occupied with one of the mechanical literary games of the new poetry—the game of trying to express one art form in terms of another.

viii. Japanese Prints

1. Aiken, Conrad. "The Return of Romanticism." Rev. of *Japanese Prints* by John Gould Fletcher. *Dial*, 65 (5 September 1918), 165-67.

   The poems are seen as slight and pleasant, but not to be

compared with *Goblins and Pagodas*. Points out that Fletcher in spite
of this book has recently been feeling his way toward a kind of
realism—an acceptance of reality, but also attempts to sublimate
reality in the process. It is Fletcher the craftsman imitating
Fletcher the poet.

2. B., W. S. "Two Poets of the Hour." Rev. of *Japanese Prints*
   by John Gould Fletcher. *Boston Evening Transcript*, 25
   September 1918, p. 6 [part II].

   A generally favorable review, noting that these poems share in
   common with Japanese poetry the tendency to exhalt the trivial
   into the realm of art. Dwells on Fletcher's preface discussion of
   Japanese poetry.

3. D., S. F. "In the Mode of Japan." Rev. of *Japanese Prints* by
   John Gould Fletcher. *New Republic*, 16 (21 September
   1918), 235, 238.

   Beyond censure because the poems bring a new note of beauty
   into American poetry. The preface is seen as a valuable aid to the
   understanding of Japanese poetry, but Fletcher's verses are
   viewed as not needing any interpretation.

4. Firkins, O. W. "Literature: Pathfinders in America."
   Rev. of *Japanese Prints* by John Gould Fletcher. *Nation*,
   108 (4 January 1919), 20-21.

   Four other books are reviewed as well. Fletcher's poems are
   seen as too formulaic. Questions whether the universal can reach
   America by way of Japan.

5. H[enderson], A[lice] C[orbin]. Rev. of *Japanese Prints* and
   The Tree of Life by John Gould Fletcher. *Poetry*, 13
   (March 1919), 340-41.

   Corbin's judgment is that these two books "in no sense
   compare with his best works." The brevity of the small poems in
   Japanese Prints and possibly their subject matter, are the only
   similarity with Japanese poetry.

6. Mencken, H. L. "Notes of a Poetry Hater." Rev. of
   Japanese Prints by John Gould Fletcher. *Smart Set*, 58
   (April 1919), 143-44.

   > Emphasizes Imagism's debt to the Japanese and the Japanese
   > debt to the Chinese. All done with characteristic Mencken wit.
   > While Mencken has relatively nice things to say about Imagism
   > and Fletcher, he does comment that at times Fletcher's poetry has
   > a clumsy artificiality because of his effort to be Japanese.

7. Rev. of *Japanese Prints* by John Gould Fletcher. *Outlook*,
   120 (6 November 1918), 382.

   > A rather nondescript review which dwells on the effects of
   > condensation and overcondensation and their relative merits and
   > demerits, respectively. The reviewer concludes that both
   > interfere with a poet's distinction of vision and style.

8. Untermeyer, Louis. "Pegasus Redivius." Rev. of *Japanese
   Prints* by John Gould Fletcher. *Yale Review*, 8 (July
   1919), 858-67.

   > Seven other books are also reviewed. Untermeyer finds that
   > *Japanese Prints* is both provocative and disappointing. Provocative
   > because of what it attempts, and disappointing because it does not
   > succeed in fulfilling its own promise or Fletcher's power.

ix. The Tree of Life

1. Aiken, Conrad. "Possession and the Possessed." Rev. of
   The Tree of Life by John Gould Fletcher. *Dial*, 66 (22
   February 1919), 189-91.

   > Views Fletcher as being his own implacable enemy. Reviews his
   > work to date and delivers a thoroughly negative assessment.
   > With the technique of the color symphonies, Aiken thinks he has
   > exhausted his technical capabilities. The symphonies are
   > language fertilized by itself rather than by thought or feeling.
   > Colorism is where Fletcher found his genre.

2. B., W. "Modern Poetry." Rev. of *The Tree of Life* and
   Goblins and Pagodas by John Gould Fletcher. *Saturday*

Review of Politics, Literature, Science and Art, 126 (9 November 1918), 1039-40.

> Finds the book as vivid as Fletcher's imagination. There is a depth behind these poems which the poet's previous volumes have lacked. To read them once is to be oppressed by the loveliness of the poems. The most arresting quality of Fletcher's work is its absolute modernity.

3. H[enderson], A[lice] C[orbin]. Rev. of *The Tree of Life* and *Japanese Prints* by John Gould Fletcher. *Poetry*, 13 (March 1919), 340-41.

> Her judgment is that neither of these books equals Fletcher's best work.

4. Rev. of *The Tree of Life* by John Gould Fletcher. *London Times Literary Supplement*, 19 September 1918, 442.

> Notes an extravagance of fancy and metaphor and abandon of love, all of which are too much. Concludes that "the true poetic impulse cannot be satisfied with regrets and repinings."

5. "The Tree of Life: Sorrows of Love Portrayed in Free Verse of John Gould Fletcher." Rev. of *The Tree of Life* by John Gould Fletcher. *Springfield Republican*, 18 May 1919, p. 19.

> Views the book's pervasive sorrow as overwhelming. The poems betray, via monotony, a lack of a sense of balance.

6. Wilkinson, Marguerite. Rev. of *The Tree of Life* by John Gould Fletcher. *New York Times Book Review*, 19 October 1919, p. 558.

> Reviewed with three other books. Wilkinson sees Fletcher as having achieved a new emotional sincerity, but loses something in his art. It is not the John Gould Fletcher whom the poetry reading public has come to expect.

x. Breakers and Granite

1. Aiken, Conrad. "Colourism in Poetry." Rev. of *Breakers*

and Granite by John Gould Fletcher. *Freeman*, 3 (6 July 1921), 405-06.

> Notes a hint of earth-mysticism in Fletcher's "miscellany of American poetry." Especially thinks well of Fletcher's experiments in polyphonic prose. Reprinted as "Fletcher, John Gould (1921)," in *A Reviewer's ABC: Collected Criticism of Conrad Aiken from 1916 to the Present*. New York: Meridian, 1958. pp. 210-13.

2. Benét, William Rose. "Amy Lowell and Other Poets." Rev. of *Breakers and Granite* by John Gould Fletcher. *Yale Review*, 11 (October 1921), 175-80.

> Nine other books also reviewed. Fletcher, along with Lowell is considered one of our finest verse pioneers. Sees Fletcher's danger as being rhetoric—too many words.

3. C., V. L. O. "The American Theme Advances." Rev. of *Breakers and Granite* by John Gould Fletcher. *Pacific Review*, 2 (September 1921), 336-41.

> Four other books are also reviewed. Regards Fletcher's effort as a failure. Observes that he is most successful in portraying the Southwest and the Mississippi.

4. Cowley, Malcolm. "These Things are Banal." Rev. of *Breakers and Granite* by John Gould Fletcher. *Dial*, 70 (June 1921), 700-04.

> Suggests that Fletcher has been led astray by his desire for infinity. Cowley's view that the book was influenced by Aiken elicited a denial from Fletcher; see *Dial*, September 1921, pp. 377-78.

5. Firkins, O. W. Rev. of *Breakers and Granite* by John Gould Fletcher. *Independent and Weekly Review*, 107 (19 November 1921), 194-96.

> The book is thought to contain some good writing and to be full of industry and misguided conscience. The experiment in polyphonic prose with its casual interior rhymes will interest the versifier. Otherwise *Breakers and Granite* is judged to be a tedious book.

6. Lowell, Amy. "Stock Taking." Rev. of *Breakers and Granite* by John Gould Fletcher. *Literary Review of the New York Evening Post*, 16 April 1921, p. 1-2.

> Finds Fletcher a man of such originality that no prototype can be found for him in the past. Tracing his growth as a poet, she praises him for having created a "vast cloudy epic of America." States that he displays no instincts for telling a story, nor does he employ wit or satire. He does have, however, an unique perception and impressions in addition to a love of color and form. Reprinted as "Stock-Taking and a Particular Instance." *Poetry and Poets*. Boston: Houghton Mifflin, 1930. pp. 137-147.

7. Sherry, Laura. "Fletcherian Colors." Rev. of *Breakers and Granite* by John Gould Fletcher. *Poetry*, 19 (December 1921), 155-57.

> Sees Fletcher as achieving a general impression of America through the combination of its various components.

8. Van Doren, Mark. "Poetic Space and Time." Rev. of *Breakers and Granite* by John Gould Fletcher. *Nation*, 112 (13 April 1921), 562.

> Calls Fletcher the most reflective of the Imagist poets who issued the 1915 manifesto. This book, however, reveals the weakness of Imagism more than it does its strengths.

9. Wilkinson, Marguerite. "Imagist Pictures of America." Rev. of *Breakers and Granite* by John Gould Fletcher. *New York Times Book Review*, 13 March 1921, p. 6.

> Views this as a dignified book which is vigorously honest, both subjectively and objectively. Fletcher knows his country well, and moreover, sees it in perspective. The reviewer would prefer poems which are somewhat more symmetrical in form but she is not adamant in her preference.

xi. Paul Gauguin: His Life and Art

1. "An American Poet Answers Paul Gauguin." Rev. of *Paul Gauguin: His Life and Art* by John Gould Fletcher.

New York Times Book Review, 11 September 1921, pp. 5, 27.

Judged a good biography as far as it goes, but it is viewed as not going far enough. Leaves much to the imagination; it will, however, serve as a good introduction to Gauguin.

2. Baury, Louis. "A Prophet in Paint." Rev. of *Paul Gauguin: His Life and Art* by John Gould Fletcher. *Freeman*, 5 (6 September 1922), 620-21.

Compliments Fletcher on making clear, in addition to Gauguin's art, the wider aspects of the man.

3. E., E. F. "Writers and Books: The Literary World of Today." Rev. of *Paul Gauguin: His Life and Art* by John Gould Fletcher. *Boston Evening Transcript*, 28 September 1921, p. 5.

Fletcher is credited with conveying a comprehensive idea of the theory and accomplishment of Gauguin's art. Four other books are also reviewed.

4. Footner, Hulbert. "The Real Gauguin." Rev. of *Paul Gauguin: His Life and Art* by John Gould Fletcher. *Literary Review of the New York Evening Post*, 8 October 1921, p. 68.

Seen as an admirable piece of work which is far too brief but nevertheless is packed with information. This first English biography of Gauguin is done with a simple and beautiful style. The most interesting thing in the book is thought to be Fletcher's inclusion of letters between Gauguin and August Strindberg.

5. Malkiel, Henrietta. Rev. of *Paul Gauguin: His Life and Art* by John Gould Fletcher. *New York Call*, 18 September 1921, p. 9.

Judges the book to be incomplete and too academic. Notes that the enthusiasm which Fletcher exhibits when writing about Gauguin's art fails to be duplicated when he is writing about the artist.

6. Mullin, Glen. "A Poet on a Painter." Rev. of *Paul Gauguin: His Life and Art* by John Gould Fletcher. *Nation*, 113 (12 October 1921), 416-18.

    Calls Fletcher's book adequate and painstaking work which will serve as a handbook to the artist. Fletcher's interpretation is viewed as suggestive and illuminating.

7. "Paul Gauguin: 'Life and Art' Described by John Gould Fletcher." Rev. of *Paul Gauguin: His Life and Art* by John Gould Fletcher. *Springfield Republican*, 6 January 1922, p. 8.

    The book is seen as straight forward and competent in its handling of Gauguin, especially his inner life.

8. Y., S. "Gauguin." Rev. of *Paul Gauguin: His Life and Art* by John Gould Fletcher. *New Republic*, 29 (22 February 1922), 377-78.

    Observes that Fletcher's achievement is that of one artist writing about another, conveying a sense of tremendous suffering, power, stoicism, pride, weakness, and energy. Finds Fletcher negligent in not dealing with the paintings themselves, but rather Gauguin's "art" in the abstract.

xii. Preludes and Symphonies

1. Grudin, Louis. "An Aesthetic Acolyte." Rev. of *Preludes and Symphonies* by John Gould Fletcher. *New York Tribune*, 28 January 1923, p. 27.

    Marks Fletcher as an influential figure in our poetry renaissance. Finds the "Preludes" yielding an effect of monotony and Oriental sadness. Sees the "Symphonies" succeeding because of ambitious and expansive form, requiring a definite thematic development. However, Fletcher fails to relate the varied vistas of his experience in the swift comprehension of small patterns.

2. ———. "A Nature Mystic." Rev. of *Preludes and Symphonies* by John Gould Fletcher. *Poetry*, 21 (February 1923), 270-75.

    Views Fletcher as looking upon the world as a vast calamity

unwinding itself toward some unimagined close, which is approached with eager apprehension. Every image is impregnated with his symbolism of the moment. Grudin categorizes Fletcher as a naturalist of the emotions.

3. Jones, Howard Mumford. "Picture Ut Poesis." Rev. of *Preludes and Symphonies* by John Gould Fletcher. *Virginia Quarterly Review*, 6 (July 1930), 472-76.

   Eleven other books are also reviewed. In a brief paragraph Jones notes that Fletcher has through intellection carried the reader far beyond the Symbolists with whom he began.

4. McClure, John. "Preludes and Symphonies by John Gould Fletcher." Rev. of *Preludes and Symphonies* by John Gould Fletcher. *Double Dealer*, 5 (January 1923), 43-44.

   Notes that the book is a reissue of two earlier books which had been written at a time when Fletcher was trying to find himself. McClure sees some fine lines mixed in with much bad poetry.

5. Pearson, Edmund Lester. "New Books and Old." Rev. of *Preludes and Symphonies* by John Gould Fletcher. *Independent Weekly Review*, 109 (16 September 1916), 136.

   Six other books of poetry are also reviewed. Fletcher's poems are thought not to bear quotation because of a pervasive triviality. This is nothing more than the notebook of a poet. There are flakes of good poetry separated by lines of banality and dull prose.

6. "Poetry." Rev. of *Preludes and Symphonies* by John Gould Fletcher. *New York Evening Post Literary Review*, 19 December 1922, p. 306.

   Seen as a subtle and unimpassioned, yet sufficiently imaginative, description to impress itself upon the memory. Calls Fletcher one of the most distinguished of the Imagists—a true craftsman.

7. Rev. of *Preludes and Symphonies* by John Gould Fletcher.
   Bookman, 56 (December 1922), 517.

   > Notes that this volume contains a musicality which is too often
   > absent in free verse. In addition, his descriptions are real. Overall,
   > however, one gets only a great inhalation of beauty with little
   > substance.

8. Warren, Austin. Rev. of *Preludes and Symphonies* by John
   Gould Fletcher. *Bookman*, 72 (September 1930), 89.

   > Within the self-imposed limitations of form and subject,
   > these poems achieve a genuine, if fragile, beauty closely
   > correspondent to the paintings of Monet and to the
   > Impressionists or to the tone-poems of Debussy. Discusses
   > Fletcher's preface in terms of its clarifying the poet's
   > earlier work.

xiii. Branches of Adam

1. Crawford, Nelson Antrim. "Philosophy in Verse." Rev.
   of *Branches of Adam* by John Gould Fletcher. *Poetry*, 31
   (January 1928), 216-18.

   > Finds that the poems have powerful imagery and symbolic
   > quality with cadences of organ music. However, it misses being a
   > powerful poem because it presents a weak argument and fails to
   > illuminate the reader on its subject of theological dualism.

2. Flint, F. S. Rev. of *Branches of Adam* by John Gould
   Fletcher. *Criterion*, 5 (January 1927), 134-36.

   > Fletcher is to be both congratulated and to be pitied, for he has
   > produced a poem that can be read with pleasure, interest, and
   > excitement, yet it is unpalatable to the contemporary audience of
   > poetry.

3. K., T. Rev. of *Branches of Adam* by John Gould Fletcher.
   Dublin Magazine, 2 (April-June 1927), 77.

   > There is much imagination in the poem, but it is not based in a
   > real imaginative life. T. K. also finds that there is a looseness of
   > form. Fletcher has made a brave attempt to pierce through an
   > inner world of reality by inadequate means. The reviewer feels
   > that artistic sanctity has been violated by the *Branches of Adam*.

4. Untermeyer, Louis. "Poets With a Difference." Rev. of *Branches of Adam* by John Gould Fletcher. *Saturday Review of Literature*, 4 (25 February 1928), 627.

   Also reviews two other volumes of poetry. Finds Fletcher's book to have an epical quality, approximating blank verse lines with a shift from ten to eighteen syllables, although it is blemished by excessive rhetoric. A success imaginatively, but a failure technically.

5. Wilson, James Southall. "American Poetry—1927." Rev. of *Branches of Adam* by John Gould Fletcher. *Virginia Quarterly Review*, 3 (October 1927), 611-14.

   Three other books are also reviewed. Wilson compares Fletcher's frankness in regard to sex with Whitman's; see pp. 613-14.

xiv. The Black Rock

1. "The Black Rock." Rev. of *The Black Rock* by John Gould Fletcher. *Boston Evening Transcript*, 21 November 1928, p. 7 [part 4].

   Fletcher has produced prose as a result of his proclivity for free verse. A rather nondescript review.

2. Gates, Barrington. "Three Poets." Rev. of *The Black Rock* by John Gould Fletcher. *Nation and Athenaeum*, 44 (3 November 1928), 182-83.

   Two other books are also reviewed. Fletcher is seen as too angry and restless to give his vision sufficient outline. Life as reflected in this book is a scatter of futile and empty movement in which men can only strive to know their own misery. The title poem is viewed as the only verse in the volume which succeeds.

3. Preston, John Hyde. "Poetry, Giants, and Lollypops [*sic*]." Rev. of *The Black Rock* by John Gould Fletcher. *Virginia Quarterly Review*, 5 (April 1929), 307-20.

   Twenty-two other books are also reviewed. Cursory remarks are made to the effect that Fletcher is a fine and very virile poet who has not "dated" as much as the other Imagists have. Preston likes Fletcher's poetry but finds the typography of the book abominable.

4.   Rev. of *The Black Rock* by John Gould Fletcher. *New Statesman*, 32 (13 October 1928), 16-17.

Reviewed with sixteen other books of poetry. Notes that Fletcher has not suffered irreparable disfigurement from his transplantation to foreign soil. Finds that Fletcher seems to be dazed and stupified by the immensity of the vista opening before him. His work is often diffuse and doudy, the effort of a poet bewildered by the brilliance of his emancipation and the multiplicity of choice it offers him.

5.   Rev. of *The Black Rock* by John Gould Fletcher. *London Times Literary Supplement*, 25 October 1928, 780.

Views Fletcher as too strident in his cynicism. The conflict which the poems embody is seen to transcend personal experience.

6.   Taylor, Rachel Annand. "Recent Poetry." Rev. of *The Black Rock* by John Gould Fletcher. *Spectator*, 141 (22 September 1928), 371-72.

Two other books are reviewed as well. Finds Fletcher's work too wordy. He is seen as Byronic in his concept of nature and attitude toward it—however he lacks the Byronic energy.

7.   Troy, William. "Lost Jehovah and Six Poets." Rev. of *The Black Rock* by John Gould Fletcher. *Bookman*, 68 (February 1929), 691-93.

Fletcher is only one of seven poets who have their books reviewed here. *The Black Rock* is viewed as being influenced by Whitman's rhapsodic mysticism, while his formal aspects are affected by the tenets of Imagism. There is a tendency to distend the image until it becomes an immense heliotrope.

8.   Van Doren, Mark. "Desperate Hope." Rev. of *The Black Rock* by John Gould Fletcher. *New York Herald Tribune Books*, 13 January 1929, p. 5.

A book of genuine—if formidable distinction is the verdict. The

reviewer remarks that this is the loneliest poetry he has ever
encountered. Sees a bit of the reformer in Fletcher, in the
tradition of Blake and Shelley.

9. Wheelright, John. Rev. of *The Black Rock* by John Gould
    Fletcher. *Hound and Horn*, 2 (July-September 1929),
    445-46.

    Fletcher's work consists of vowel quality and cadence, and a
    intermittent sense for images. He sometimes displays his art in
    conjunction with his message, but as he never delivers his
    message in his art, his poems may be said not to exist.

10. Zabel, M[orton] D. "Dust Discrowned." Rev. of *The
    Black Rock* by John Gould Fletcher. *Poetry*, 33 (January
    1929), 222-24.

    Points out that Fletcher and Amy Lowell were the first
    Imagists to waiver from the Imagist doctrine. Views Fletcher
    as being chiefly concerned with evolutionary faith beyond
    negation.

xv. John Smith—Also Pocahontas

1. B., M. Rev. of *John Smith—Also Pocahontas* by John Gould
    Fletcher. *Outlook and Independent*, 150 (12 December
    1928), 1332-33.

    Views Fletcher's presentation as shattering some long standing
    illusions about Smith. Rather cursory treatment along with five
    other books reviewed.

2. Finger, Charles J. "Books About Heroes: Prince Charlie,
    Capt. Smith, and Sergt. York." Rev. of *John Smith—
    Also Pocahontas* by John Gould Fletcher. *New York World*,
    28 October 1928, p. 8E.

    Admires the human qualities with which Fletcher imbued his
    hero. Smith as Fletcher portrays him is no stuffed shirt or painted
    puppet, nor is he the adventurer with all unscrupulous deeds
    glossed over. Two other books are also reviewed.

3. MacDonald, William. "The Grandfather of Virginia."
   Rev. of *John Smith—Also Pocahontas* by John Gould
   Fletcher. *New York Herald Tribune Books*, 16 December
   1928, p. 16.

   Judges the book to be a judicious rendering of history. Focuses
   on Fletcher's attempt to dedeify Smith in order to suit the public's
   supposed postwar demand for verity. The cost is a humorless
   book.

4. Rev. of *John Smith—Also Pocahontas* by John Gould
   Fletcher. *Nation*, 127 (12 December 1928), 665.

   Sees nothing new in this book to make it a particularly valuable
   contribution to scholarship.

5. Riorden, M. M. "Fletcher Bares Captain Smith." Rev. of
   John Smith—Also Pocahontas by John Gould Fletcher. *New
   York Evening Post*, 1 December 1928, p. 9M.

   Finds the book somewhat dull because of Fletcher's un-
   imaginative matter-of-fact treatment of his hero.

xvi. The Crisis of the Film

1. Wagenknecht, Edward. "The Movies Versus the
   Talkies." Rev. of *The Crisis of the Film* by John Gould
   Fletcher. *Yale Review*, 19 (March 1930), 637-39.

   Also reviewed is *The Movies and the Talkies* by Gilbert Seldes.
   Finds Fletcher's aesthetic interests betray him in his desire to rule
   out all dramatic interest and merely make the film a symphony of
   pictures.

xvii. The Two Frontiers: A Study in Historical Psychology

1. Bakeless, John. Rev. of *The Two Frontiers: A Study in
   Historical Psychology* by John Gould Fletcher. *New York
   Evening Post*, 15 February 1930, p. 10.

   Views the book as intelligent yet inaccurate and not very
   profound. Judges Fletcher's thesis as more than merely alarmist

because it is based in a humanism that is at once scientific and aesthetic.

2. Baltzly, Alexander. "The Two Frontiers." Rev. of *The Two Frontiers: A Study in Historical Psychology* by John Gould Fletcher. *Current History and Forum*, 32 (June 1930), 604-05.

> Dwells on the inaccuracies of Fletcher's treatise. Sees value in the contrast between Russian and American minds. The book is full of suggestiveness, often is sensitive, even brilliant, but Fletcher is not content with imitating—he forces his data into a preconceived scheme.

3. Carter, John. "America and Russia As Seen in Recent Books." Rev. of *The Two Frontiers: A Study in Historical Psychology* by John Gould Fletcher. *Outlook and Independent*, 154 (26 February 1930), 352, 356.

> Puts Fletcher's book in the context of a debate with other current books on the topic which are also reviewed here.

4. Cowley, Malcolm. "Ford or Lenin." Rev. of *The Two Frontiers: A Study in Historical Psychology* by John Gould Fletcher. *New York Herald Tribune Books*, 9 February 1930, p. 19.

> Notes that Fletcher's "vast historical synthesis" is founded on questionable and contradictory beliefs. Cowley dismisses Fletcher's prediction that a great war between Russia and the United States will destroy civilization. Sees Fletcher's method as a dangerous progeny of Oswald Spengler.

5. Grattan, C. Hartley. "Unity and Disunity." Rev. of *The Two Frontiers: A Study in Historical Psychology* by John Gould Fletcher. *New Freeman*, 1 (4 June 1930), 285-86.

> Views Fletcher's book as "romantic complaining." Finds the author oppressed by the disunity of the world, producing a poor social diagnosis via a faulty method.

6. Freeman, Joseph. "Views of Soviet Russia." Rev. of *The Two Frontiers: A Study in Historical Psychology* by John Gould Fletcher. *Virginia Quarterly Review*, 6 (July 1930), 442-49.

   Three other books are also reviewed. Notes that Fletcher's is a strongly philosophic work influenced by Spengler. The reviewer suggests that Fletcher's facts need to be checked out, and also points out a lack of insight into the importance of specific national and class cultures.

7. H., B. "The Two Frontiers." Rev. of *The Two Frontiers: A Study in Historical Psychology* by John Gould Fletcher. *Boston Evening Transcript*, 15 March 1930, p. 3.

   Fletcher is complimented for his omission of any "ultra-modern thought tendencies" in the two countries about which he writes. The reviewer notes that Russia and the United States are more alike than some of our super-patriots would like to think. An extremely interesting book which draws some very unpleasant conclusions.

8. Josephson, Matthew. "Russian-American Chimera." Rev. of *The Two Frontiers: A Study in Historical Psychology* by John Gould Fletcher. *Nation*, 130 (16 April 1930), 462.

   Views the book as rich in prophecy, analogy, fantasy, and sheer nonsense. Fletcher's *Two Frontiers* falls into the category of works of synthesis. Finds Fletcher lost in the historical ocean.

9. Strumsky, Simeon. "Contrasting the Civilizations of Russia and America." Rev. of *The Two Frontiers: A Study in Historical Psychology* by John Gould Fletcher. *New York Times Book Review*, 9 March 1930, p. 2.

   To the extent that Fletcher has established his thesis he has done it by patient, conscientious spade work. However, the facts are there to be marshalled against him if the case demands it.

10. Tate, Allen. "The Twin Monsters." Rev. of *The Two Frontiers: A Study in Historical Psychology* by John Gould

Fletcher. *New Republic*, 62 (19 March 1930), 132.

> Finds the book both provocative and profound. It is not
> formally documented history and therefore ought not to be
> criticized as such—there is a good deal of valuable criticism of
> American culture thrown off by the way. Tate thinks the book a
> prose "Wasteland."

xviii. XXIV Elegies

1. Benét, William Rose. "Contemporary Poetry." Rev. of
   XXIV Elegies by John Gould Fletcher. *Saturday Review of
   Literature*, 5 October 1935, p. 42.

   > Praises Fletcher's technique. The fluidity and flexibility which is
   > achieved avoids monotony while imaginatively expressing a
   > profound pessimism.

2. Blackmur, R. P. "Versions of Fletcher." Rev. of *XXIV
   Elegies* by John Gould Fletcher. *Poetry*, 47 (March 1936),
   344-47.

   > "It is the old question, with Mr. Fletcher, of how much
   > intention can outrun ability, how much feeling can replace
   > the . . . form. . . ." Fletcher falters because of the relationship
   > between language and theme. "His poems are not objects but
   > media." An important analysis of Fletcher's work.

3. F., I. Rev. of *XXIV Elegies* by John Gould Fletcher.
   Christian Science Monitor, 30 August 1935, p. 14.

   > Emphasizes Fletcher's range of subject and vision—a
   > panoramic poet.

4. Gregory, Horace. "Hours in a Poet's Life Cycle." Rev. of
   XXIV Elegies by John Gould Fletcher. *New York Herald
   Tribune Books*, 29 December 1935, p. 6.

   > States that Fletcher's imagery is now accompanied by formal
   > music. Gregory views this collection as considerably better than
   > the *Symphonies* and the *Irradiations* upon which Fletcher's
   > reputation had been based. The imprint of the lesser Symbolists
   > is seen in Fletcher's work.

5. Jack, Peter Munro. Rev. of *XXIV Elegies* by John Gould
    Fletcher. *New York Times Book Review*, 12 January 1936,
    p. 15.

    Although much of Fletcher's earlier irridescence is gone, it has
    been supplanted by a maturity in which the development of
    thought, in detail and imagery, is paramount.

6. Pearce, T. M. "Rockefeller Center in the Camino." Rev.
    of *XXIV Elegies* by John Gould Fletcher. *New Mexico
    Quarterly Review*, 5 (May 1935), 84-87.

    Pearce focuses on the strange combination of urbanism and
    regionalism which is apparent in this volume.

7. Rev. of *XXIV Elegies* by John Gould Fletcher. *Nation*, 141
    (2 October 1935), 391.

    The book is seen as lacking method which is not compensated
    for by its curiosity. There is a dearth of clear central impression,
    and the poems do not embody a coherent attitude toward
    experience. Fletcher is seen as being minutely interested in the
    world and highly perplexed by it.

8. Untermeyer, Louis. "The New Poetry." Rev. of
    XXIV Elegies by John Gould Fletcher. *American Mercury*,
    36 (November 1935), 377-80.

    Reads the significance of "24" as being one poem for each of the
    day's hours. Only a short space (p. 378) is devoted to Fletcher. By
    and large this review is of all new poetry books which have
    appeared during the year.

9. Zabel, Morton D. Rev. of *XXIV Elegies* by John Gould
    Fletcher. *New Republic*, 85 (8 January 1936), 263-64.

    Notes that Fletcher's early work had been influenced by the
    Imagists. Fletcher's poetry has matured in his more recent work—
    as exemplified by *XXIV Elegies*. Fletcher's struggle as an artist
    clearly lies between his poetic enthusiasms of the Imagist period
    and his later convictions about the age in which he lives, its
    traditions, and his personal responsibilities toward them. In some
    of the poems the influence of Imagism is still recognizable and the
    elegiac tone, after a while, becomes enervating.

xix. Life Is My Song

1. Colum, Mary M. "Courageous Living." Rev. of *Life Is My Song* by John Gould Fletcher. *Forum*, 99 (January 1938), 22-23.

    Colum's focus on Fletcher's first marriage is interesting. Overall she views this autobiography to be the account of a brave man, who sacrificed much for what he believed to be the pursuit of spiritual truth.

2. Fulkerson, Baucum. "John Gould Fletcher." Rev. of *Life Is My Song* and *Selected Poems* by John Gould Fletcher. *Sewanee Review*, 46 (July-September 1938), [275]-88.

    An examination of Fletcher's creative evolution from an Imagist to a regionalist.

3. Jack, Peter Munro. "John Gould Fletcher: The Imagist and the Man." Rev. of *Life Is My Song* by John Gould Fletcher. *New York Times Book Review*, 5 December 1937, pp. 33, 35.

    The reviewer can find no warmth in the writing, yet it serves as a painstaking literary history. It is also viewed as a sometimes embarrassing portrait of a poet "who has somehow never pulled his weight." Jack's final verdict is that Fletcher's indecision has led him to affiliate with too many movements, and inevitably weakened any chances for real impact in a literary or social sense.

4. Kreymborg, Alfred. "A Poet's Story." Rev. of *Life Is My Song* by John Gould Fletcher. *New Republic*, 93 (17 November 1937), 53-54.

    Sees the book as earnest and impassioned because its author is quite aware of the world to which his being responds. Kreymborg notes that there are several blind spots in Fletcher's narrative.

5. Pearce, T. M. Rev. of *Life Is My Song* and *Selected Poems* by John Gould Fletcher. *New Mexico Quarterly Review*, 8 (November 1938), 268-70.

    Basically an overview of Fletcher's Imagist beginnings with an interesting anecdote regarding Aldington's inability to understand Walt Whitman. More is said about Fletcher's life than about the book which is being reviewed.

6. Quinn, Kerker. "From Little Rock to London." Rev. of *Life Is My Song* by John Gould Fletcher. *New York Herald Tribune: The Lively Arts and Book Review*, 21 November 1937, p. 2.

Fletcher's narrative skill is seldom on a par with his descriptive prose. There is a natural inclination to take himself and his work too seriously, to the point where the reviewer finds it bordering on triviality.

7. R[itchey], J[ohn]. "A Poet Sings the Song of His Life." Rev. of *Life Is My Song* by John Gould Fletcher. *Christian Science Monitor Weekly Magazine*, 15 December 1937, p. 11.

Credits Fletcher with being a rare creature in a modern mechanized world, a professional poet.

8. Walton, Eda Lou. "A Sad Song." Rev. of *Life Is My Song* by John Gould Fletcher. *Nation*, 145 (25 December 1937), 723-24.

Views the whole book as the complaint of a man at odds with his world. Notes that Fletcher's relations with women point toward an Oedipus complex. Concludes that Fletcher was a romanticist who found life unromantic.

xx. Selected Poems

1. Deutsch, Babette. "Lost Address." Rev. of *Selected Poems* by John Gould Fletcher. *Poetry*, 52 (September 1938), 347-51.

States that while interested in technical experiments of the Imagist group, Fletcher cared little for the principles of the group. Deutsch finds this book flawed by the poet's failure to declare himself rather than by the creativeness of his execution.

2. Finch, John. Rev. of *Selected Poems* by John Gould Fletcher. *New Republic*, 95 (29 June 1938), 224, 226.

> What is seen as emerging from this volume is the line of the poet's career, "twisting over twenty-five years, represented, to head, at the end, in a direction opposite from its beginning." Finds Fletcher's later adherence to meter and rhyme as being clumsy.

3. F[itts], D[udley]. "The New Books: Poetry." Rev. of *Selected Poems* by John Gould Fletcher. *Saturday Review of Literature*, 27 August 1938, p. 21.

> Other books are also reviewed. The literary historian will need Fletcher's book for his consideration of the Imagist movement, and the philosophical critic will be interested in it as a record of how the revolutionary passes into commonplace. Fitts finds the book, as a whole, confusing.

4. Fulkerson, Baucum. "John Gould Fletcher." Rev. of *Selected Poems* and *Life Is My Song* by John Gould Fletcher. *Sewanee Review*, 46 (July-September 1938), [275]-88.

> An examination of Fletcher's creative evolution from an Imagist to a regionalist.

5. Holmes, John. Rev. of *Selected Poems* by John Gould Fletcher. *Atlantic*, 162 (October 1938), [n. p.].

> Sees Fletcher's style as perfected from Imagism so that now it is richer with color, warmer with emotion. This book is seen as representing a very important poet in the pantheon of modern poetry.

6. Pearce, T. M. Rev. of *Selected Poems* and *Life Is My Song* by John Gould Fletcher. *New Mexico Quarterly Review*, 8 (November 1938), 268-70.

> Fletcher writes poetry which is a tapestry of the rich imagery of the mind and eye. Views Fletcher's "occasional" pessimism as the mood of the realist rather than that of the escapist or dreamer.

7. Rev. of *Selected Poems* by John Gould Fletcher. *New York Herald Tribune Books*, 12 June 1938, p. 17.

> Raises the question that perhaps Fletcher lived too long in England. Judges that the poems of the late Twenties and early Thirties are clearly superior to the earlier Imagist poems written during the poet's expatriation.

8. R[itchey], J[ohn]. "Mr. Fletcher Shows His Verse." Rev. of *Selected Poems* by John Gould Fletcher. *Christian Science Monitor Weekly Magazine Section*, 29 June 1938, p. 10.

> Views Fletcher as a sensory poet. Notes that Fletcher is a poet by intention, which may explain the sensory nature of his poetry. Not much poetry which emotionally moves the reader, but there is much craftsmanship to appreciate.

xxi. South Star

1. Allsopp, Fred W. Rev. of *South Star* by John Gould Fletcher. *Arkansas Historical Quarterly*, 1 (March 1942), 78-83.

> The book is seen as an important contribution to the artistic literature of Arkansas. The reviewer notes Fletcher's move away from Imagism to a more conventional style.

2. Brown, Harry. "The South in His Mouth." Rev. of *South Star* by John Gould Fletcher. *Voices*, 106 (Summer 1941), 53-55.

> "A turkey of a book. A lemon of a book. Oh, a lemon." Finds the book dull in the reading and evidently careless in the writing. A scathingly negative review, not only in regard to Fletcher, but also in regard to Southern regionalism.

3. Clark, Axton. "A New Collection of Poems by John Gould Fletcher." Rev. of *South Star* by John Gould Fletcher. *New York Times Book Review*, 11 May 1941, p. 4.

> Fletcher's technical accomplishment emerges throughout in his control of the variety of meters and in the richness of his perception. This in spite of a diffuseness and repetiveness of expression. A sense of origin and belonging saturates the book.

4. D[rew], E[lizabeth]. Rev. of *South Star* by John Gould
   Fletcher. *Atlantic*, 168 (September 1941), [n. p.].
   > Considers these poems of revery. The poems are historical, but
   > it is not history lighted by any fresh poetic vision. It is expressed
   > at a sustained level of adequacy, never surprising, never sinking
   > below competence.

5. Frankenberg, Lloyd. "Wild Sea Water." Rev. of *South Star*
   by John Gould Fletcher. *Nation*, 152 (14 June 1941),
   704.
   > The reviewer is complimentary of the exotic diction and
   > permutations of various mood movements. The orchestration is
   > seen as being marred by the apparent belief that anytime any
   > theme is repeated and expanded enough it grows in significance.

6. Quinn, Kerker. "Story of an Arkansas Poet." Rev. of
   South Star by John Gould Fletcher. *Poetry*, 58
   (September 1941), 334-36.
   > Sees Fletcher as being prone to lapse into "obviousness." In
   > addition, he has become increasingly didactic.

7. Rev. of *South Star* by John Gould Fletcher. *Springfield
   Republican*, 20 April 1941, p. 7E.
   > Finds Fletcher the master of his subject because he is a part of
   > his environment.

8. Ritchey, John. "John Gould Fletcher, New Style." Rev.
   of *South Star* by John Gould Fletcher. *Christian Science
   Monitor Weekly Magazine Section*, 24 May 1941, p. 10.
   > Sees little of Fletcher's earlier style and manner because a
   > conventional mode of expression is used. This is the work of a
   > poetic mind in transition is Richey's verdict. Fletcher is viewed as
   > "uncomfortable" in rhyme and as a result lapses too often into
   > pedestrian contrivances.

9. Sweeny, John L. Rev. of *South Star* by John Gould
   Fletcher. *Yale Review*, 30 (Summer 1941), 817-22.
   > Ten other books of poetry are also reviewed. Short
   > and cursory treatment of Fletcher. Views the book as

something like history but not feeling like it. The work is too pedestrian, unconvincing when Fletcher's view of nature is overdramatized.

10. Untermeyer, Louis. "Richness and Restraint." Rev. of *South Star* by John Gould Fletcher. *Saturday Review of Literature*, 19 July 1941, p. 6.

Two other books are also reviewed. Fletcher's book is found to be haphazard in style, and sprawling in construction. The reviewer shows more appreciation for the regionalist poetry in the second half of the volume.

xxii. The Burning Mountain

1. Fairchild, Donald. "Sense and Music in Lines of John Gould Fletcher." Rev. of *The Burning Mountain* by John Gould Fletcher. *Chicago Sun Book Week*, 7 July 1946, p. 5.

On the whole this is not to be considered an impressive book. The reviewer sees some, but very little, growth of expression— mostly evident in the lines on snow and about Spain. Finds this volume failing and succeeding in equal measures.

2. Freemantle, Anne. Rev. of *The Burning Mountain* by John Gould Fletcher. *Commonweal*, 44 (4 October 1946), 601-02.

Four other books are also reviewed. Fletcher is accused of not always having something to say, but rather dealing only in affect. Views Fletcher as a poet "whose true metier is the American interior, inland United States, the land itself, the feel and meaning of it."

3. Holmes, John. "New Books of Verse." Rev. of *The Burning Mountain* by John Gould Fletcher. *New York Times Book Review*, 29 September 1946, p. 22.

Two other books are also reviewed. Compliments Fletcher on his powerful sense of the old space and quest for the essence of the Southwest, as well as his mature realization of the vastness of time. Considers "Journey Day" the crown of Fletcher's writing career. Fletcher is to be viewed as an important figure in American poetry.

4. Humphries, Rolfe. Rev. of *The Burning Mountain* by John
    Gould Fletcher. *Nation*, 163 (17 August 1946), 189-90.

    Regrets that the poet has failed to create music in spite of using
    musical forms. Views *The Burning Mountain* and the two other
    books reviewed with it as literary inflation.

5. Lechlitner, Ruth. "American Background." Rev. of *The
    Burning Mountain* by John Gould Fletcher. *New York
    Herald Tribune Weekly Book Review*, 15 September 1946,
    p. 16.

    The poetry of Fletcher has little resemblance to his early
    Imagist work. Only the skeleton of the original structure
    remains. A conservative moralistic tone is infused throughout,
    while displaying an amazing disregard for form and subject and
    good craftsmanship. Content has taken over as the prime
    consideration.

6. MacLow, Jackson. "Three Books and a Marvel." Rev. of
    The Burning Mountain by John Gould Fletcher. *Western
    Review*, 11 (Spring 1947), 190-92.

    Three other books are also reviewed. Only one paragraph is
    devoted to *The Burning Mountain*. "The marvel" is William Carlos
    Williams's *Patterson*.

7. Manchester, William. "Two Books of Poetry." Rev. of
    The Burning Mountain by John Gould Fletcher. *Springfield
    Republican*, 3 August 1946, p. 4.

    One other book is also reviewed. Finds Fletcher's volume to be
    worth reading in spite of the melodramatic tendencies exhibited
    and the sometimes exaggerated symbolism.

8. S., P. P. "Poet-Historian." Rev. of *The Burning Mountain*
    by John Gould Fletcher. *Christian Science Monitor*, 8 July
    1946, p. 16.

    These poems are thought to be like a clear mirror, catching and
    giving back, without confusion the strange scenery of the past
    eight years. The reviewer compliments Fletcher's workmanship,
    and notes the Imagist influence.

9. Snell, George. "Fletcher's *Burning Mountain* and Other
   New Books of Poetry." Rev. of *The Burning Mountain* by
   John Gould Fletcher. *San Francisco Chronicle: This World*,
   11 August 1946, p. 15.

   Finds Fletcher particularly adept at creating the mood of the
   landscape and recreating a sense of the American past.

10. Squires, James Radcliffe. Rev. of *The Burning Mountain*
    by John Gould Fletcher. *Chicago Review*, 1 (Summer
    1946), 172-73.

    The introductory paragraph of this review is an acidic attack on
    Imagism. Views Fletcher as, technically, the same Imagist whom
    the coterie minds of the 20s adored. Fletcher's technique is seen
    merely to be saying "look-what-beauty-I-see." Then the poet
    defines and redefines. But beauty, Squires assures us, like a joke,
    becomes tedious with explanation.

11. Webster, Harvey Curtis. "Music vs. Eloquence." Rev.
    of *The Burning Mountain* by John Gould Fletcher. *Poetry*,
    69 (March 1947), 353-56.

    Webster is impressed by the intelligence with which Fletcher
    displays "his occasional hope and frequent despair." Fletcher is in
    accord with the insights of such poets as Auden, Eliot, and Yeats.
    Unfortunately, Fletcher does not phrase his intelligence as vividly
    as these poets do. The constant reversion to cliché has made
    Fletcher less memorable than any other modern poet who has
    deserved popular distinction.

xxiii. Arkansas

1. Craven, Avery. "The Story of a Unique State." Rev. of
   Arkansas by John Gould Fletcher. *New York Herald
   Tribune Weekly Book Review*, 15 July 1947, p. 2.

   Unsurpassable for reader who would know the state of
   Arkansas, both as a state of mind and a state of the union. The
   story is told with affection, humor, and much courage.

2. Frederick, John T. "A Poet's Picture of His Native

Arkansas." Rev. of *Arkansas* by John Gould Fletcher. *Chicago Sun Book Week*, 8 June 1947, p. 4.

Finds the book fresh, informative, and good entertainment. A notable addition to the regional literature of the nation. Fletcher's narrative is presented with the poet's concreteness and selection of detail.

3. H., R. M. Rev. of *Arkansas* by John Gould Fletcher. *Christian Science Monitor Magazine Section*, 28 June 1947, p. 11.

A review which analyzes the points which Fletcher wishes to make and how he goes about making them. Notes Fletcher's observation that the South declined spiritually since the Civil War, since the only progress made was material in nature. Overall, the portrait of Arkansas which Fletcher paints is viewed as temperate, judicial, and selective rather than comprehensive.

4. Lawson, James R. Rev. of *Arkansas* by John Gould Fletcher. *Southern Folklore Quarterly*, 11 (September 1947), 230-31.

A favorable review which points out that Fletcher deals in hard facts but does not ignore the "folk" aspects of the state's history. Considers Fletcher quite qualified to write the state's history since his family played a part in its settlement.

5. McDonald, Gerald D. Rev. of *Arkansas* by John Gould Fletcher. *Library Journal*, 72 (15 May 1947), 805.

Notes that there is some good material on local festivals and holidays. While based on careful research and reliable sources, the book has been written for popular reading, with particular relish for the anecdote.

6. Reiser, Robert E. Rev. of *Arkansas* by John Gould Fletcher. *Arkansas Historical Quarterly*, 6 (Summer 1947), 204-06.

The best short history of the state. "While not scholarly, the book is representative of the highest type of popular historical literature."

7. Reynolds, Horace. "Portrait of the Wonder State." Rev. of *Arkansas* by John Gould Fletcher. *Saturday Review of Literature*, 7 June 1947, p. 22.

> Views Fletcher's history as an unreserved, almost somber but clear portrait of a confused and ebullient region. He has done everything but explain why Arkansas fascinates us.

8. Thistlewaite, Frank. "Border State." Rev. of *Arkansas* by John Gould Fletcher. *Spectator*, 179 (17 October 1947), 504, 506.

> Fletcher's natural feeling for his subject and his talent as a writer have resulted in a popular history of considerable quality. The reviewer finds the more recent history of the state less vivid than the earlier.

9. Worley, Ted R. Rev. of *Arkansas* by John Gould Fletcher. *Mississippi Valley Historical Review*, 34 (March 1948), 660-61.

> Judges that the volume deserves a high place in popular historical literature. The volume is boldly interpretive. The defects of the book are attributable more to the status of historical knowledge in certain areas than to the author.

10. Young, Marguerite. "A Pair of Arkansas Travelers." Rev. of *Arkansas* by John Gould Fletcher. *New York Times Book Review*, 15 June 1947, p. 7.

> Another book on Arkansas is also reviewed. Finds Fletcher's book fascinating reading. There is a suggestion Fletcher has broken out of stereotype.

III. Indexes

Note: The Index of Names lists all proper names found in the text, including those which occur as parts of titles of books. The Index of Titles lists all of Fletcher's works, all secondary works, the titles of books in which secondary essays appear, and the titles of the journals in which reviews of Fletcher's works appear. Boldface type in the Title Index and the Name Index indicates that the item appears in the main bibliographic entry.

A. Index of Names

Abel, Lionel. I-C-2.
Aiken, Conrad. I-B-41, 70, **89**, 103, **193, 203, 318, 406**; II-B-**1, 2, 3, 4**, 66; II-C-vi-**1**, viii-**1**, ix-**1**.
Alden, Raymond M. II-C-vi-**2**.
Aldington, Richard. I-B-**34, 35,** 66, **140, 304**.
Aldis, Mary. I-B-**45**.
Aldrich, Ann Rochelle. II-B-**5**.
Allen, Charles. II-B-**34**.
Allen, Hervey. I-B-**188**.
Allsopp, Fred W. II-C-xxi-**1**.
Anderson, J. Redwood. I-B-**243**.
Armstrong, Archibald T. I-B-**156**.
Arvin, Newton. I-B-**375**.
Auden, W. H. I-B-**302**, 442; II-C-xxii-11.
Austin, Mary. I-B-**188**.

B., M. II-C-xv-**1**.
B., W. II-C-vii-**1**, ix-**2**.
Bakst, Leon. I-A-3.
Bakeless, John. II-C-xvii-**1**.
Baltzly, Alexander. II-C-xvii-**2**.
Barfield, Owen. I-B-**258**.
Baudelaire, Charles. I-A-2, 5; I-B-44, 464.

Bauer, Marion. I-D-1.
Baury, Louis. II-C-xi-**2**.
Beach, Bernard. I-B-**294**.
Beatty, Richmond Croom. I-B-**418**.
Beaudoin, Kenneth Lawrence. II-B-**6**.
Beaumont, C. W. I-B-**83**.
Behrens, Ralph. II-B-**7**.
Bellaman, Henry. I-B-**193**.
Benét, Stephen Vincent. I-B-**185, 405, 442**.
Benét, William Rose. II-C-x-**2**, xviii-**1**.
Berryman, John. I-B-**413**.
Bess, Demaree. II-B-**8**.
Bianchi, Martha Dickinson. I-B-**207**.
Bianchi, Ruggero. II-B-**9**.
Bingham, Millicent Todd. I-B-**429**.
Binyon, Lawrence. I-B-**406**.
Black, John. I-B-**129**.
Blackmur, R. P. II-C-xviii-**2**.
Blake, William. I-B-**55**, 118, 137, 192, **206**, 464; II-C-viii-**8**, x-**2**, xvi-**1**, xxi-**9**.

165

B. Index of Titles